Reconsidering Cultural Heritage in East Asia

Edited by
Akira Matsuda and Luisa Elena Mengoni

]u[

ubiquity press
London

Published by
Ubiquity Press Ltd.
6 Windmill Street
London W1T 2JB
www.ubiquitypress.com

First published 2016

Cover design by Amber MacKay
Front cover image: Sainsbury Institute for the Study of Japanese Arts and Cultures
Background cover image: geralt / Pixabay

Printed in the UK by Lightning Source Ltd.
Print and digital versions typeset by Siliconchips Services Ltd.

ISBN (Paperback): 978-1-909188-88-4
ISBN (PDF): 978-1-909188-89-1
ISBN (EPUB): 978-1-909188-90-7
ISBN (Mobi/Kindle): 978-1-909188-91-4

DOI: http://dx.doi.org/10.5334/baz

The full text of this book has been peer-reviewed to ensure high academic standards. For full review policies, see http://www.ubiquitypress.com/

Suggested citation:
Matsuda, A and Mengoni, L E (eds.) 2016 *Reconsidering Cultural Heritage in East Asia*. London: Ubiquity Press. DOI: http://dx.doi.org/10.5334/baz. License: CC-BY 4.0

To read the free, open access version of this book online, visit http://dx.doi.org/10.5334/baz or scan this QR code with your mobile device:

Contents

Acknowledgements v

Contributors vii

Introduction: reconsidering cultural heritage in East Asia (Akira Matsuda and Luisa Elena Mengoni) 1

Considering undercurrents in Japanese cultural heritage management: the logic of actualisation and the preservation of the present (Masahiro Ogino) 15

Evolving and contested cultural heritage in China: the rural heritagescape (Marina Svensson) 31

The emergence of 'cultural heritage' in modern China: a historical and legal perspective (Guolong Lai) 47

Ethnic heritage in Yunnan: contradictions and challenges (Fuquan Yang) 87

Cultural heritage in Korea – from a Japanese perspective (Toshio Asakura) 103

The concept of 'cultural landscapes' in relation to the historic port town of Tomo (Kazuo Mouri) 121

Shaping Japan's disaster heritage (Megan Good) 139

Acknowledgements

This book has its origin in the workshop and conference 'Cultural Heritage? in East Asia', organized by the Sainsbury Institute for the Study of Japanese Arts and Cultures (SISJAC), the Japan Foundation and the International Centre for Chinese Heritage and Archaeology, with support from the School of World Art Studies and Museology, University of East Anglia, the Victoria and Albert Museum and the UCL Institute of Archaeology, in London and Norwich in March 2010. The event commemorated the tenth anniversary of the foundation of SISJAC.

The success of the event led to the publication of this book. Some of the papers delivered at the workshop and conference were rewritten for the book, while others were specially commissioned to prompt a wider consideration of issues in cultural heritage in East Asia.

We express our heartfelt thanks to SISJAC, without the generous support of which neither the event nor this book could have been materialized. We dedicate this book to SISJAC.

We would also like to thank the authors of the individual contributions for their great patience while this book has been prepared. We acknowledge the comments offered by the two anonymous reviewers, which helped us improve the book.

Contributors

Toshio Asakura is a Professor at Ritsumeikan University and Professor Emeritus at the National Museum of Ethnology in Japan. He has published extensively on social structures in East Asia, in particular Korea and Japan. He has been undertaking a long-term comparative research project on culinary culture in Korea and was awarded the Ok-gwan (Jewelled Crown) Order of Cultural Merit of the Republic of Korea in 2013.

Yang Fuquan is Professor at the Yunnan Academy of Social Sciences, Vice President of the Association of Chinese Ethnology and the President of the Association of Yunnan for Naxi Studies. He is an expert on Chinese ethnic history with a focus on Naxi studies and has published extensively. His publications include *Stories in Modern Naxi* (VGH Wissenshaftsverlag 1988), *A Study of Dongba Religion (Dongba jia tong lun)* (Zhonghua shu ju 2012) and *A Study on Suicide for Love among the Naxi People (Yu long qing shang: Naxi zu de xun qing yan jiu)* (Yunnan renmin chubanshe 2008).

Megan Good is an independent researcher in the field of heritage studies with a particular focus on Japan. She earned her BA from the University of North Carolina at Chapel Hill and her MA from the University of East Anglia.

Guolong Lai is a member of the School of Historical Studies, Institute for Advanced Study (2014–2015) and Associate Professor of Chinese Art and Archaeology at University of Florida. He earned a BA in International Law at Jilin University in China, an MA in Chinese Archaeology and Paleography at Beijing University and a PhD in Chinese Art History at the University of California, Los Angeles. Dr Lai has worked as a graduate intern and served as Consultant to the China projects at the Getty Conservation Institute in Los Angeles. He recently contributed to and co-edited *Collectors, Collections & Collecting the Arts of China* (University Press of Florida 2014), a volume based on a symposium that he organized. He has published extensively on early Chinese bronzes and mortuary culture. He is the author of *Excavating the Afterlife: The Archaeology of Early Chinese Religion* (University of Washington Press 2015).

Akira Matsuda is an Associate Professor at the Department of Cultural Resources Studies, the University of Tokyo. He earned his PhD in public archaeology at University College London and is an Academic Associate at the Sainsbury Institute for the Study of Japanese Arts and Cultures. He serves as the Secretary of the World Archaeological Congress. His research focuses on the meaning, (re)presentation and use of the past in contemporary society.

Luisa Elena Mengoni is Head of the V&A Gallery, Shekou and currently based in Shenzhen, where she coordinates the collaboration between the V&A and China Merchants Shekou. She formerly worked as a curator of Chinese art at the V&A and consultant on heritage projects in China. Holding a PhD in Chinese archaeology from University College London (UCL), she published on identity and ethnicity, Chinese export art and collecting history. Her current research interests focus on new developments of Chinese design and crafts, and the emergence of new museum models and creative hubs in China.

Kazuo Mouri is a researcher and writer with a strong interest in cultural heritage in Japan, especially site and landscape conservation. Previously he was a journalist at NHK (Japanese Broadcasting Corporation) and served as its senior commentator specialising in cultural properties. Presently he is the Director of the Institute of Port-Town Culture in Setouchi.

Masahiro Ogino is a Professor of Sociology at Kwansei Gakuin University. He earned a PhD in Sociology from the University of Paris VII. His research interests are focused on the sociology of culture, the study of capitalism and the history of social theory. He has served as the President of La Société Franco-Japonaise de Sociologie since 2004. In addition to his publications in Japanese, he has published two books in French. One book concerns the Great Hanshin Earthquake (*Fissures* 1998); the other is a study of a small village in France (*Un Japonais en Haute-Marne* 2011). His second Japanese book, a study of fraud, has been translated into English (*Scams and Sweeteners* 2007).

Marina Svensson is Professor of Modern China Studies at the Centre for East and South-East Asian Studies, Lund University. Her research focuses on human rights, legal issues, cultural heritage debates and practices, documentary film and media and communication studies. Her major publications include *Debating Human Rights in China: A Conceptual and Political History* (2002), and she co-edited books such as *The Chinese Human Rights Reader* (co-edited with Stephen Angle 2001), *Gender Equality, Citizenship and Human Rights: Controversies and Challenges in China and the Nordic Countries* (co-edited with Pauline Stoltz, Sun Zhongxin and Qi Wang 2010), *Making Law Work: Chinese Laws in Context* (co-edited with Mattias Burell 2011) and *Chinese Investigative Journalists' Dreams: Agency, Autonomy, and Voice* (co-edited with Elin Sæther and Zhi'an Zhang 2013).

Introduction: reconsidering cultural heritage in East Asia

Akira Matsuda* and Luisa Elena Mengoni†
*University of Tokyo
†Victoria and Albert Museum

The seven chapters of this book examine a range of issues related to cultural heritage in East Asia, including perspectives from the fields of anthropology, ethnology, sociology and art history. While these contributions reflect the different disciplinary backgrounds of the authors, there is one element that pertains to all of them: they do not regard cultural heritage as a given but rather as something that is made and being constantly remade. The book as a whole can therefore be understood to consider how cultural heritage is conceptualised, materialised, experienced and negotiated

How to cite this book chapter:
Matsuda, A and Mengoni, L E 2016 Introduction: reconsidering cultural heritage in East Asia. In: Matsuda, A and Mengoni, L E (eds.) *Reconsidering Cultural Heritage in East Asia*, Pp. 1–13. London: Ubiquity Press. DOI: http://dx.doi.org/10.5334/baz.a.

in various cultural, political and social contexts in East Asia. This approach – to view cultural heritage as a construct or a process – is not new and has already been at the heart of 'heritage studies' for over a decade (Byrne 2008; Harvey 2001; Smith 2006). What characterises this book, however, is that it applies the approach to cultural heritage in East Asia, an area which has tended not to be extensively explored and critically scrutinised. While for the purpose of this book East Asia is represented by Japan, China and Korea, in future it would be desirable to extend the scope of examination to include other neighbouring countries.

Differentiation and assimilation of heritage in East Asia

As with other geographically defined notions of cultural heritage, such as Western European heritage and African heritage, cultural heritage in East Asia tends to be understood in terms of its local specific manifestations, thus emphasising its difference from heritage in other regions. Its commonly recognised expressions are often related to certain distinctive cultural and social aspects, such as Confucian values, Daoist philosophy, Buddhist religious practices, languages based on ideograms and the use of specific local resources and technologies. This is of course unavoidable to some degree, since cultural heritage is closely associated with peoples' identities, which is in part predicated on the idea of how a group of people is different from others. The underlying logic here is that different groups of people identify with different expressions of heritage. Such a logic often leads to an 'exoticised' notion of cultural heritage, conceptualised through selection for representation vis-à-vis other countries and regions (see Gupta & Fergusson 1992). The same logic can also result into simplified narratives, particularly when one attempts to interpret influences, integrations or hybrid and complex material manifestations of heritage.

Seeing heritage as solely a marker of difference is, however, limiting because it can not only exoticise and/or simplify a culture, but also essentialise it: highly recognisable exotic aspects of cultural heritage tend to be understood as fixed and unchangeable in people's imagination (Sahlins 1993). Both outside observers and local people can be complicit in this process. For example, locals may 'strategically essentialise' their own culture by portraying their heritage as exotic to outsiders in order to gain more recognition (Spivak 1988; Sylvain 2005). In fact, what we regard as 'cultural heritage' often results from a web of interactions and exchanges between various groups and has been changing and reconstructed over time by all the actors involved.

Thinking of cultural heritage as a marker of difference is limiting also because it discourages the understanding of how the heritage of one place can be similar to the heritage of another place. Just as people's group identity is predicated on *both* how a group is different from others *and* how the members of the same group share common traits, cultural heritage of a place is conceptualised not only in terms of how it is different from heritage elsewhere *but also* in terms of what commonalities are shared amongst a variety of heritage expressions existing in that place. In other words, in people's imagination, geographically defined cultural heritage assimilates differences within itself. For example, despite the commonly accepted understanding that there is a variety of cultural heritage expressions across Japan, most people are ready to talk about 'Japanese heritage'; they hardly doubt that the notion of 'Japanese heritage' is impossible. This points to the need of investigating how the imagined notion of 'Japanese heritage' is able to assimilate the diversity of local differences within

Japan, making people believe that there is a similarity of heritage practices and manifestations across Japan. The same can be said of 'Chinese heritage' and 'Korean heritage', and also of 'East Asian heritage'. When we talk about 'East Asian heritage', we assume, naturally and uncritically, that differences between and across Japanese, Chinese and Korean heritage can somehow be subsumed under the notion of 'East Asian heritage'. This of course can be a problematic and politically dangerous assumption, but is also unavoidable to certain extent because the very nature of cultural heritage is not only to divide but also unite. Seeing cultural heritage only as a marker of difference is limiting in this sense.

Leading on from this idea, we wish to encourage the reader to consider how the dual and dialectical mechanism of differentiation and assimilation of heritage operates in East Asia, both at the level of each country and of the region as a whole. On the one hand, there is a need to understand how the notions of Japanese, Chinese and Korean heritage assimilate differences within each country to propose a unified concept, and likewise, how the notion of East Asian heritage assimilates differences within the region. On the other hand, it is also necessary to examine the tension and dissonance caused by the assimilation of differences, which could lead to the unsettling and re-conceptualisation of existing notions of heritage.

It is also relevant to consider how heritage notions can be transformed and re-negotiated by the actors involved, depending on their agendas and aspirations. A number of chapters in the book address such dialectic shaping and reshaping of cultural heritage. Svensson's chapter (Chapter 3), for example, examines the tension related to the way in which halls where rural lineage-based practices traditionally take place in China have been designated officially and used increasingly for tourism, while also continuing to act as places for local ancestral worship. Against the background of rapid economic growth nationwide, the Chinese government is both tightening/regulating and internationalising its management of cultural heritage, as it can serve as a symbol of national pride, global prestige and as a resource for tourism development. The 'authorized heritage discourse' (Smith 2006) that underpins such governmental initiatives is dominant and is gradually transforming rural cultural practices into official heritage, causing conflict with the local discourse that has traditionally been sustaining customs of ancestor worship.

Yang (Chapter 5) also looks into the tension caused by different understandings and uses of cultural heritage in China, analysing the relationship between tourism development and local practices related to ethnic heritage. The rapid expansion of tourism in Yunnan province is increasingly changing customs and lifestyles of the Naxi and Moso ethnic groups, and one can see how their cultural heritage, both tangible and intangible, is gradually staged and used to attract more tourists. Yet, just as globalisation spurs localisation as a reaction (Featherstone 1995: 94–97; Harvey 1989: 302–303), the commodification of ethnic heritage has urged Naxi and Moso communities to take new initiatives to regain control over its management and representation.

Asakura's chapter (Chapter 6), examining cultural heritage in Korea from a Japanese comparative perspective, includes an analysis of the 'making' of Korean and Japanese food. He contends that the Korean government has in recent years been actively involved in the authentication and promotion of Korean food, whereas in Japan similar matters concerning Japanese food have traditionally been and still are dealt with by private initiatives. The 'Japan–Korea Kimchi War' – which Asakura mentions as an example of the Korean government's attempt to strengthen the brand of Korean food internationally – is interesting in that it illustrates the nation's claim as the owner of 'national food'. The fact that Kimchi has been appreciated in the international market regardless of the consumers' knowledge of whether it is made in Korea or Japan suggests that it could potentially be considered as 'East Asian food'. And yet, the dissonance within East Asia – in this case, between Korea and Japan – makes Kimchi distinctly Korean, and thus does not easily confer on it the status of 'East Asian heritage'.

Temporality of heritage

Another theme that we wish to highlight in this book is the temporality of heritage, that is to say, the ways in which cultural heritage represents time or is related to conceptions of time. Ogino addresses this theme most directly in his chapter (Chapter 2) by discussing the discourse of cultural heritage management in Japan. He considers two different modes of the temporality of heritage in Japan. Using the term 'the logic of actualisation' he first argues that there has been a tradition in Japan that the past is 'brought up to date' in the present through the medium of cultural heritage. He contrasts this tradition with the linear notion of time upon which the Western concept of heritage and museums largely rest. He contends that the logic of actualisation has been a solution to the difficulty of connecting the pre-modern past of Japan to the future envisioned by modernity, the latter being effectively a concept imported from the West.

Ogino then draws our attention to another mode of the temporality of heritage – the preservation of the present. He argues that people living in late modern societies are increasingly seeing themselves as an object to be perceived from an external world, while at the same time they, as a subject, engage with their own world in everyday life. This 'doubling of the world', he argues, accounts for the proliferation of the preservation of the present: we are getting to see the present world as if it were already heritage to be archived and safeguarded.

What deserves particular attention in Ogino's argument is that while his logic of actualisation is discussed in relation to Japan, the preservation of the present is observable not only in Japan but in late modern societies across the globe. This raises an interesting question as to whether the logic of actualisation applies also to China and Korea, which have equally been faced with the challenge of reconciling tradition and modernity since the 19th-century. Lai's investigation (Chapter 4) of the social and political circumstances in which the state legislation for the protection of cultural relics was established in the early period of the Republic of China (1912–49) is relevant here, since attempts to construct Chinese heritage – or the transformation of 'cultural property' of imperial and private ownership into public and state-owned 'cultural heritage' – occurred as China began modernising itself. Lai contends that the national system for the protection of cultural relics was established on the one hand due to China's modernisation and the introduction of Western values and disciplines, and on the other hand in the context of the removal of ancient relics from China by Westerners.

Good (Chapter 8) discusses how social memories of devastating earthquakes have been passed down in Japan. Her main focus is on the preservation of materials damaged by the 2011 Great East Japan Earthquake and Tsunami, which is a striking example of the preservation of the present. It is noteworthy that immediately after the catastrophic tsunami there were already calls for preserving damaged ruins in the stricken areas. As Good explains, there were opinions both for and against such calls. Some local residents objected to the idea of preserving ruins as monuments because they wanted to move on with their own lives, and with the recovery of their communities, without being constantly reminded of the painful experience of the tsunami. The argument for the preservation of the ruins, on the other hand, stressed the importance of remembering the disaster and passing on the lessons learned from it to future generations, so that the damage caused by similar disasters could be prevented or mitigated in the future. While both opinions are understandable, there is clearly a modernist undertone in the pro-preservation opinion – human society should, and can, reduce the risk of natural disaster. The idea expressed by some of the pro-preservation group members to link the preserved 'disaster heritage' to tourism development is also uncompromisingly modernist: heritage is regarded here as a resource to capitalise on. One can thus argue that attempts to preserve ruins resulting from the 2011 Great East Japan Earthquake and Tsunami as 'disaster heritage' were an extreme manifestation of modernity: ordinary materials that were part of people's everyday world yesterday can become ruins that have social and educational value today, going on to be preserved, commemorated and used as heritage tomorrow.

Terminology of heritage

A final theme that we wish to address in this book is the body of terms involved in and used to discuss the 'making' of cultural heritage in East Asia. Language is at the core of constructing meaning, and the making of heritage depends on, and is conditioned by, terminology. In Britain, for example, the term 'heritage' came into full use in official language from about 1975 (Larkham 1999: 115–116) and in people's everyday language from about the early

1980s – this broadly coincided with the emergence of the 'heritage discourse', prompted by the adoption of UNESCO's World Heritage Convention in 1972 and the establishment of English Heritage in 1983. Previously, people used more specific terms – 'monuments', 'historic buildings', 'archaeological sites', 'works of art' or 'relics' for example – referring to components of what we mean today by 'cultural heritage'. One can thus infer that people identified with the past through a variety of means, which, however, remained conceptually discrete since there was no overall notion of 'cultural heritage' that could integrate them.

The heritage discourse beginning from about the 1980s has subsequently gradually developed, not only in Britain but globally, and this has come to require new, more complex terminology. While the initial range of terms used to describe the categories of cultural heritage was more or less limited to 'architectural heritage' and 'archaeological heritage', or 'national heritage', 'local heritage' and 'World Heritage', it has since diversified greatly. Today in heritage studies there are discussions of 'intangible heritage' (Smith & Nakagawa 2009; see also Ogino's Chapter 2, Svensson's Chapter 3, Fuquan's Chapter 5 and Asakura's Chapter 6), 'industrial heritage' (Douet 2012; Oevermann & Mieg 2014), 'urban heritage' (Lorgan 2002), 'ethnic heritage' (Hendersson 2003), 'living heritage' (Stovel et al. 2005), 'maritime heritage' (Laurier 1998), 'difficult heritage' (Macdonald 2009) and so on. All of these categories can, of course, apply to cultural heritage in East Asia, and it would also be possible to add more categories to refine the conceptualisation of heritage further. In this book, for example, Good (Chapter 8) discusses the term/concept of 'disaster heritage'.

Two chapters in the book address the making of terminology related to cultural heritage in East Asia more directly. Mouri

(Chapter 7) examines the extent to which the term/concept of 'cultural landscape' has been accepted in Japan through a case study of Tomo, a port town with a historic landscape that was recently threatened by the proposal to construct a bridge. He first compares UNESCO's definition of 'Cultural Landscape' with three similar and yet slightly different categories of cultural properties in Japan – and one must note here that in Japan 'cultural properties' is the term legally and administratively employed to refer to cultural heritage (Matsuda 2014: 4156). It is notable that the Japanese term '*bunkateki keikan*' is a direct translation of the English 'cultural landscape', and yet it still differs from UNESCO's 'Cultural Landscape'. Mouri argues that this difference can be explained by the pre-existence of other related categories of cultural properties in Japan: in particular, *meishô* and *dentôteki kenzôbutsugun hozon chiku*. *Meishô*, a traditional term/concept that has existed in Japan much longer than 'cultural landscape', is essentially a 'culturally appreciated place', and as such is different from 'cultural landscape' which is defined in terms of the history of human interactions with a place as can be read from its visual appearance. In other words, the visual appearance matters more in a 'cultural landscape' than in a *meishô*. This demonstrates that both 'cultural landscape' and *meishô* are culture-specific concepts, at least in their origin.

Lai (Chapter 4) scrutinises the legal and historical documents related to the process of establishing the national system for protecting cultural heritage in early 20th-century China. This process began by legally defining what cultural heritage is, and one can note here the first uses of a particular terminology. Lai explains that the terms/concepts such as *guwu* (ancient relics), *shiji* (historic sites), *guji* (ancient sites), *mingsheng* (famous sights), *wenwu* (cultural relics) and *guobao* (national treasure) all came into use during this period, which marked 'the birth of modern China' – these new terms being necessary in order to legally transform imperial collections into state properties.

Finally, from a cross-regional perspective it is worth noting that the Japanese, Chinese and Korean translations for the English 'cultural heritage' – '*wenhua yichan*', '*bunka isan*' and '*munhwayusan*', respectively – became popular only from about the 1980s and the early 1990s (see Lai Chapter 4 for '*wenhua yichan*', and Matsuda 2013: 23–24 for '*bunka isan*'). This is probably the result of the widespread adoption of the so-called 'internationally recognised standards' developed and advocated by UNESCO and other international organisations across the World; China, for example, ratified the UNESCO's World Heritage Convention in 1985, and Japan accepted it in 1992 and the Republic of Korea in 1988. Such a recent and rapid acquisition of the heritage concept can be connected to the need of East Asian countries to align themselves to the international scene and engage more actively with their own cultural heritage as a strategy to manage the portrayal and use of their respective pasts in a coherent and programmatic fashion.

However, as a number of the chapters in this book suggest, cultural heritage is fundamentally fluid and never subject to total control by any institution. It would therefore be unproductive to consider what exactly constitutes 'Japanese heritage', 'Chinese heritage', 'Korean heritage' or 'East Asian heritage' – such questioning is promised not to yield a complete, satisfactory answer. Far more constructive will be, instead, to examine how and why different actors in East Asia employ and deploy the notion of heritage on each relevant occasion, with multiple dynamics and strategies at play – this is exactly what we wish to propose in this book. Ultimately, reconsidering cultural heritage in East Asia is necessary not so much because we need to understand what East Asian heritage precisely is, but because we need to understand how people 'go about' cultural heritage in East Asia.

References

Byrne, D 2008 Heritage as Social Action. In: Fairclough, G, Harrison, R, Jameson, J H Jr and Schofield, J (eds.) *The Heritage Reader*. Abingdon and New York: Routledge. pp. 149–173.

Douet, J (ed.) 2012 *Industrial Heritage Re-tooled: The TICCIH guide to Industrial Heritage Conservation*. Lancaster: Carnegie.

Featherstone, M 1995 *Undoing Culture*. London, Thousand Oaks and New Delhi: Sage.

Gupta, A and Ferguson, J 1997 Beyond "Culture": Space, Identity, and the Politics of Difference. *Cultural Anthropology*, 7: 6–23.

Harvey, D 1989 *The Condition of Postmodernity: An Enquiry into the Origins of Cultural Change*. Oxford: Blackwell.

Harvey, D C 2001 Heritage Pasts and Heritage Presents: Temporality, Meaning and the Scope of Heritage Studies. *International Journal of Heritage Studies*, 7 (4): 319–338.

Henderson, J 2003 Ethnic Heritage as a Tourist Attraction: The Peranakans of Singapore. *International Journal of Heritage Studies*, 9 (1): 27–44.

Larkham, P 1999 Preservation, Conservation and Heritage: Developing Concepts and Applications. In: Cullingworth, B (ed.) *British Planning: 50 Years of Urban and Regional Policy*. London: Athlone Press. pp. 105–122.

Laurier, E 1998 Replication and Restoration: Ways of Making Maritime Heritage. *Journal of Material Culture*, 3 (1): 21–50.

Logan, W S 2002 *The Disappearing 'Asian' City: Protecting Asia's Urban Heritage in a Globalizing World*. Hong Kong: Oxford University Press.

Macdonald, S 2009 *Difficult Heritage: Negotiating the Nazi Past in Nuremberg and Beyond*. London and New York: Routledge.

Matsuda, A 2013 Paburikku Akeorojî No Kanten Kara Mita Kôkogaku, Bunkazai, Bunkaisan (Archaeology, Buried

Cultural Properties and Cultural Heritage as Seen from the Viewpoint of Public Archaeology). *Quarterly of Archaeological Studies (Kôkogaku Kenkyû)*, 60 (2): 19–33.

Matsuda, A 2014 Japan: Cultural Heritage Management. In: Smith, C (ed.) *Encyclopaedia of Global Archaeology*. New York: Springer. pp. 4156–4160.

Oevermann, H and Mieg, H A (eds.) 2014 *Industrial Heritage Sites in Transformation: Clash of Discourses*. New York: Routledge.

Sahlins, M 1993 Goodby to Tristes Tropes: Ethnography in the Context of Modern World. History. *Journal of Modern History*, 65 (1): 1–25.

Smith, L 2006 *The Uses of Heritage*. London: Routledge.

Smith, L and Akagawa, N (eds.) 2009 *Intangible Heritage*. London: Routledge.

Spivak, G 1988 Subaltern Studies: Deconstructing Historiography. In: Guha, R. and Spivak, G. (eds.) *Other Worlds: Essays in Cultural Politics*. Oxford: Oxford University Press. pp. 197–221.

Stovel, H, Stanley-Price, N and Killick, R (eds.) 2005 *Conservation of Living Religious Heritage*. Rome: ICCROM.

Sylvain, R 2005 Disorderly Development: Globalization and the Idea of "Culture" in the Kalahari. *American Ethnologist*, 32 (3): 354–370.

Considering undercurrents in Japanese cultural heritage management: the logic of actualisation and the preservation of the present

Masahiro Ogino
Kwansei Gakuin University

The aim of this chapter is to analyse two undercurrents in Japanese cultural heritage management. The first of these is the 'logic of actualisation', or the way in which the past is brought up to date in the present. This is a long-standing traditional approach towards the

How to cite this book chapter:
Ogino, M 2016 Considering undercurrents in Japanese cultural heritage management: the logic of actualisation and the preservation of the present. In: Matsuda, A and Mengoni, L E (eds.) *Reconsidering Cultural Heritage in East Asia*, Pp. 15–29. London: Ubiquity Press. DOI: http://dx.doi.org/10.5334/baz.b.

past in Japan, and also helps distinguish Japanese cultural heritage management from approaches taken in Europe. The other undercurrent is a recent phenomenon that can be observed not only in Japan but also in many other late-modern societies across the World: that is, the preservation of the present. Examining these two undercurrents helps us understand the particular situation in which Japan finds itself today in terms of cultural heritage management.

The logic of actualisation

In Europe, people's conception of time seems in part informed by the presence of historic monuments and museums. In this cultural context, many old buildings retain their original use and function socially as monuments. These monuments, through their very presence, visually represent history in its continuity, and people thus come to acknowledge a linear notion of time by seeing them in their everyday life. There are also many museums in Europe; in fact, the very concept of the museum first emerged in European countries. These museums collect and display old objects, or antiquities, that are otherwise inaccessible to the public, and by so doing deprive these objects of their original use and grant them a status as historic items. Museum objects thus become more than just embodiments of the past, since they actively instil the concept of linear history in the observer's mind.

> 'Museums are primarily intended for objects that do not belong to us. They come from far back in the past, and we have inherited them from previous generations, and our first duty is to pass them down intact to those who will come after us' (Chiva & Levi-Strauss 1992: 170)

This statement by Chiva and Levi-Strauss highlights on the one hand the nature of 'uprooted' objects, whose purpose is to show history in its duration and continuity, and on the other the role of the museum as the institutional scene of their preservation.

In Japan, historic monuments and museums also exist. However, there has been a different conceptualisation of time there. The past is instead brought up to date in the present – such conceptualisation of time, which I wish to call 'the logic of actualisation', seems to underpin the way in which Japan manages its cultural heritage. In order to understand how the logic of actualisation applies to Japanese cultural heritage management, it is helpful to examine what outside observers often consider to be a characteristic of Japanese heritage preservation: the concept of 'Living National Treasures' (Aikawa-Faure 2014: 39–44).

The term 'Living National Treasures' is used informally to refer to what the Japanese Law for the Protection of Cultural Properties defines as 'Holders of Important Intangible Cultural Properties'. Although the two terms are often used interchangeably, they actually have different connotations. The legal term does not refer to people – agents, practitioners, or artists – but rather to the arts and crafts themselves as traditions. This is because the purpose of the law is not to honour living artists, but to preserve their crafts or habitus, which are intangible. The informal term 'Living National Treasure', on the contrary, refers to the artist, the 'living' person. The fact that the term 'Living National Treasure' is more commonly used in people's everyday language than 'Holders of Important Intangible Cultural Properties' is quite telling: the informal term seems to fit better with the Japanese notion of art and tradition.

Whoever speaks of a Living National Treasure supports the view that tradition does not dwell within finished works, but rather within works in the making. In this sense, practicing traditional art is not aimed at faithfully preserving the heritage of the past, but at bringing what is deemed to have existed in the past to the present. Seen from this angle, tradition as such can be seen to no longer exist. Even if one concedes that tradition does exist, it is invisible and must be made manifest in order to be recognised. This non-materialistic view of tradition is better represented by theatre than by any other forms of traditional art. When an actor designated as a Living National Treasure performs on stage, tradition is made manifest through his/her individual acting. Tradition does not have any fixed embodiment here – it remains invisible until it is staged, and is made present and visible by and through Living National Treasures. In other words, the traditional becomes *actualised.* Theatrical performance is thus a form of heritage exhibition, achieved through publicly recognised actors and musicians (see also Jackson & Kidd 2011).

This logic of actualisation of tradition also applies to other forms of traditional art in Japan. Bizen pottery is a good example. What characterises Bizen pottery is that it is never glazed; its famous natural beauty makes it a popular choice for the tea ceremony, which promotes simple and unadorned beauty (*wabi*) (Rousmaniere 2007: 158). The pottery producing town of Bizen, which has existed since the 12th-century, is today a flourishing community and industry, with around four hundred potters running their shops next to their kilns. The success of Bizen as a pottery town, however, was not always secure. Bizen pottery went through a long period of stagnation, especially after its production lost the support of the regional authority in Okayama in 1868, caused by the collapse of the Edo political system. According to the brochure published by the Bizen Pottery Traditional and Contemporary Art Museum, Tôyô Kaneshige, son of a long dynasty of ceramists, revived the Bizen tradition and was awarded the title of Living National Treasure in 1956. The Bizen pottery crisis, which had lasted from the late 1860s through to the 1950s, was resolved thanks to the passion and determination of the individual artist Kaneshige (Rousmaniere 2007: 170). After his death in 1967, however, Bizen found itself without a Living National Treasure, and part of its heritage was lost again. For the next three years, no ceramicist worthy of the title of Living National Treasure emerged in Bizen. In 1970, an artist by the name of Kei Fujiwara was however nominated a Living National Treasure (Rousmaniere 2007: 168), and then in 1987, four years after Fujiwara's death, Tôshû Yamamoto became the next title holder. On each occasion the title of Living National Treasure was conferred it was seen as a crucial event through which heritage is passed on. The history of Bizen pottery is thus represented by Living National Treasures who are believed to embody the Bizen artistic tradition. This tradition is not embodied by the works of art but by the people who produce them. Here one can recognise the logic of actualisation – the past is not transmitted through the conservation of objects, but is maintained, or kept alive, by people.

The fate of historic objects and monuments

Rather than present the past through preserved objects, Living National Treasures enable a continual revival of what existed in the past. According to the logic of actualisation, the conservation of works is secondary to their creators. Nevertheless, some objects and buildings have stood the test of time. How does Japanese cultural policy deal with these?

In much of Europe, history is seen through preserved objects. These objects are visible and, whenever possible, publicly displayed. Indeed, one of the social functions – and responsibilities – of museums is to make the past visible by showing ancient objects. For example, the paintings on display in the Pantheon show Paris, the eternal city, rescued time and time again from repeated invasions; these paintings symbolically represent Paris as a city stubbornly intent on preserving the past. In fact, Europe appears to me, a Japanese, to be making extraordinary efforts to protect historic objects and monuments from the affronts of time. I am even tempted to assert that the arch-enemy of Europe is not some foreign invader, but time itself.

The situation is quite different in Japan. There are not many surviving historic monuments, largely due to the fact that most traditional architecture is made from wood, which decays relatively quickly. Even more significantly, historic objects are often removed from public view. According to the logic of actualisation, there is no need for objects to act as guarantors of linear history. Even if one wishes to preserve them, this is not made obvious to the public. The example of Shôsôin, an extremely rare historic treasure house originating in the Nara period (710–794), clearly shows the relative lack of interest amongst the Japanese in making historic objects visible. Shôsôin houses about 9,000 artefacts, including objects offered on the occasion of the inauguration of the giant statue of Buddha at Tôdai-ji temple in 752. The Shôsôin treasures remained uncatalogued until the end of the 19th-century, when, in 1892, the Imperial Household Ministry finally took charge of their management (Tokyo kokuritsu hakubutsukan 1973: 380). Today most of the treasures are kept in storerooms, built after the Second World War to ensure the best possible conservation. The public has access to only part of them, and at no other time than during the annual exhibition (for seventeen days) held in the Nara National Museum (Nara National Museum 2014). Therefore, the conservation and exhibition of the treasures occupy two distinct spaces, both physically and symbolically.

The exhibition of the treasures can be compared to an actor walking onto a stage. The treasures are normally invisible, and their secrets are unveiled only when they are performed on stage: that is, when they are on display each year. Such invisibility endows objects with a mysterious aura. In the display, the public discovers highly rare, even exotic items, rather than *historic* objects that have been passed down the generations. Those objects are not there to represent the past, but as reminders that they are still in the present, albeit hidden most of the time. The same logic applies to many historic buildings. In Kyoto, for example, palaces and many temples open only on certain days. This occasional opening reminds people that the monuments are still being used, and even inhabited, in the present day. The public thus discovers a world removed in space from everyday life, and in this special space tradition is actualised – or brought into the present. The admittance of the public to a secret world through an occasional opening is sustained by the logic of actualisation.

Historic buildings are kept away from people's everyday life even more manifestly at the Museum Meiji-mura in Aichi prefecture (Graburn 2008: 229–233). Meiji-mura, on the shores of Lake Iruka, is an open air museum about one million square metres in area. Visitors walk through a small forest before discovering another world, in which the Meiji period (1868–1910) springs back to life. The museum houses over 60 buildings from the Meiji period, all of which have been restored to their original condition. All types of buildings have been re-erected in the village: town halls, banks, hospitals, factories, schools, public baths, a hairdresser's, a church, a cathedral, and even the Kanazawa jail, complete with cells open to visitors. The Shinagawa lighthouse, one of the oldest in Japan, erected in 1870, looks onto Lake Iruka. A little further on, one finds the railway bridge that once crossed the River Rokugô in Kanagawa. Even buildings used by emigrants have been brought here: for example, a meeting hall from Hilo in Hawaii (1889) and a Japanese emigrant's house from Brazil. Some of the buildings still fulfil their former functions, such as the Ujiyamada Post Office, built in 1909 in Ise, where visitors can mail postcards. In the Kureha-za Theatre, built in 1868, they can watch a performance of Kabuki theatre. The restaurant of the Oi butcher's (1887) serves a beef dish known as *sukiyaki.* A Kyoto tramway and two steam locomotives (one imported from Britain in 1874, the other from the United States in 1912) carry visitors to and fro through the centre of the village.

Meiji-mura is unique inasmuch as all the buildings there were originally built in the Meiji period, a period characterised by modernisation and an opening to the outside world. Almost all of Meiji-mura reconstructions relate to modernity, which was viewed at the time as synonymous with Western civilisation: the hospital, factory, school, railway and so forth. The Meiji government had built the Shinagawa lighthouse as part of an agreement with signatories of the 1858 Treaties of Amity and Commerce. Its building was therefore strongly linked to the opening up of Japan to the West, without which neither the church nor the cathedral could possibly have been built. The policy behind the Museum Meiji-mura also represents changes in daily life: the *sukiyaki* is more than a simple meat dish; it reflects a change in Japanese eating habits, which did not normally include beef in pre-Meiji times. The 'Western style' hairdresser's was another such novelty.

Meiji-mura aims to save Meiji buildings which might otherwise completely disappear; urbanisation has indeed already destroyed many buildings from that period. Meiji-mura is a way of recovering this almost lost time, now materialised on the shores of Lake Iruka. This materialisation of the past in an isolated space sends the message that the past does not precede the present – it is simply *elsewhere.*

As seen in the above examples, there seems to be a reluctance to represent linear time in Japanese cultural heritage. Arguably, this reluctance stems from the absence of the very concept of linear time in pre-Meiji times, and reflects Japan's embarrassment in the face of modern civilisation during the Meiji period. In the grand project of modernisation, Japan needed to follow the West as bearers of the future, even though this was not a future originally conceived by Japan. Initially it must have felt impossible to establish any continuity between, say, ancient Bizen vases and locomotives imported from the West. And yet, for the ancient Bizen vases to acquire any *historic* value that was worthy of preservation, the Japanese needed to believe that the locomotives were *theirs* – this is because the modern concept of, and desire for, material conservation is predicated on the linear notion of time: from the past, through the present, to the future.

The initial response to the irresistible rise of modernization, and ultimately Westernization, in Meiji Japan was a negation of their past. Many traditional buildings, objects, and customs were abandoned surprisingly rapidly and easily, as exemplified by the nationwide destruction of Buddhist temples and castles in the early Meiji period. When the Japanese subsequently realised that their ancient objects were actually worthy of preservation because of their *historical* value, even though they could not be easily connected to the future envisaged by the ongoing project of modernisation, they started setting them aside and preserving them, just like the Shôsôin treasures which were not publicly displayed until 1940.

The logic of actualisation then offered a solution to the deadlock between tradition and a largely imported modernity. According to this logic, tradition is no longer part of the past – it exists in the present, in the same way as industrial products. In this sense, the Meiji architecture restored in Meiji-mura – which strives to adapt modern architecture to the environment of a bygone Japan – is for the Japanese a somewhat nostalgic symbol of the attempt at reconciliation of tradition and modernity.

The preservation of the present

Let us now turn to the second undercurrent in Japanese cultural heritage management – the preservation of the present. The phenomenon of preserving the present is not unique to Japan, and is in fact present in many late-modern societies across the globe (Hartog 2005). What we are talking of here is heritage of the past that is so recent that people feel it to be almost a part of the present. Examples of the preservation of the present abound: 'industrial heritage' has recently been adopted as a new category of cultural heritage (Douet 2011), and objects and sites of the twentieth century, and even 21st-century, have been increasingly preserved as cultural heritage.

The root cause of the preservation of the present can be found in the loss of traditional 'sacred centres', which used to link people with the world of the unknown, a world inhabited by the ancestors and spirits: for example, mountains inhabited by deities, temples, and palaces (Eliade 1969). In many late-modern societies, locations where people can symbolically interact with deities and ancestral spirits have steadily disappeared. In the case of Japan, modernisation starting from the Meiji period has seen the destruction of many Buddhist temples, shrines, castles, and other historic buildings in order to make way for more Westernised structures and places. The loss of these former sacred centres has given rise to two developments. On the one hand, people's aims and desires become more directed towards 'transitional' places, such as shopping centres and tourist destinations. On the other hand, when people experience such transitional places - which are by definition outside their everyday lives - they start seeing the world to which they return as something external, and moreover they begin to behave in accordance with previously external views and desires. These two developments create an unstable situation in which people feel they are in two places at once - the world they live in and the world they visit. This condition of drifting back and forth between the two worlds can be called 'the doubling of the world' (*sekai no nijû-ka*).

Those who live in famous tourist destinations experience this doubling of the world on a daily basis: the place where they spend their daily lives is at the same time a destination where tourists continuously arrive. A typical example of this in Japan can be found in Shukunegi on Sado Island. Shukunegi was formerly a base for the shipping industry in Japan, and its downtown area still retains a characteristic historical atmosphere. In 1991 the area was nationally designated an Important Preservation District for Groups of Traditional Buildings. The interiors of one section of the buildings in the district are now open to the public. For the purposes of display, the modernised interiors were largely restored to their traditional form. Many people actually continue to live in the area. Certain houses have the highly distinctive shape of the prow of a ship. They are called *sankakuya* (triangle houses) and always feature in tourist guidebooks. An elderly woman living alone in one such house has said, however, 'The word *sankakuya* is made up' (author personal communication) and stressed how constraining it is to live in the preservation district. In fact, people who reside in the preservation district are not even at liberty to renovate their own dwellings, since they must conform to the regulations imposed by the Law for the Protection of Cultural Properties. For these residents, their own home has at the same time become a transitional location where tourists come and gather. When residents realised that they had no choice but to accept these outsiders for economic reasons, they formulated systems of accepting them; they developed plans for living with the doubling of the world, one example being the production of tourist-oriented folk crafts.

When the doubling of the world becomes very strong, people start having the urge to preserve the present as heritage – that is to say, to preserve the world they live in. The most common form of preserving the present can be observed in the trend to treat incidents or pressing social issues as the subject of preservation and display. For example, immediately after the Great Hanshin Earthquake of 1995, a movement got underway to designate the active fault under Awaji Island, which caused the earthquake, as a natural monument. Three years after the disaster, the national government designated the fault as a natural monument, and the Nojima Fault Preservation Museum was opened on the site of the fault. At the same time, a destroyed house was named the 'memorial house' and became an object of preservation. A similar phenomenon was also observed after the devastating tsunami caused by the 2011 Great East Japan Earthquake: almost immediately after the devastation, a series of campaigns emerged to preserve damaged structures and other remains as monuments (see Good's chapter in this book).

Yet, the desire to preserve the present goes beyond historical events such as disasters to include even daily life. An exhibit at the Matsudo Municipal Museum recreates a section of modern urban industrial housing. The subject of the display is the Tokiwadaira Danchi (Apartment), originally built in 1961. From around the period of the 1960s, large apartment complexes similar to the Tokiwadaira Danchi were constructed across Japan, in both urban areas and rural areas near cities. These apartment complexes transformed not only the Japanese living environment, but the entire Japanese way of life, including culinary customs. This is readily understood by considering the so-called '2DK' type of *danchi* apartment. The term '2DK' designates a standard apartment with two bedrooms, a dining room, and a kitchen. The kitchen is fitted with modern conveniences, a space entirely different from the dark dirt-floor kitchens found in previous Japanese homes. The Matsudo Municipal Museum has recreated a model of the 2DK apartment, with a period refrigerator, television, and Western-style lounge set. Nowadays a refrigerator, television, and washing machine can be found in every home as daily necessities, but in the early 1960s they were together called the 'Three Sacred Treasures', symbolising the modernization of daily life. There is absolutely nothing remarkable about either the 2DK model or the style of life that it has promoted. Based on the standards of previous museums, one would hardly suppose it would become the subject of preservation. People still live at the Tokiwadaira Danchi, and yet part of it has been recreated to show how it used to look in the 1960s.

Museums were already places where oddities and low-value objects were put on display, but today familiar things such as household electric appliances still in use in everyday apartment life have become objects intended for preservation. This trend is emerging at a time when society has lost its traditional sacred centres and starts searching for new centres to be put on display as a self-portrait of the present. This is a narcissistic form of display, born of a desire to preserve the present. At Shukunegi, old buildings are still inhabited and simultaneously used as cultural heritage to be shown to tourists. In the case of Matsudo Municipal Museum, common everyday elements of the present, or near past, are being turned into a self-expressive form of heritage. Both forms of the preservation of the past were triggered by the doubling of the world – we are increasingly seeing the world we live in as cultural heritage.

Conclusion

In this chapter I have examined two undercurrents in Japanese cultural heritage management: the logic of actualisation and the preservation of the present. The two undercurrents are concerned with different temporal consciousness. One seeks to bring the past up to date in the present and the other seeks to preserve the present as if it were heritage of a distant past. The two undercurrents are also different in terms of whether they are specific to Japan or part of a more global phenomenon. The logic of actualisation is specific to Japan, as it originated from pre-modernisation era Japan and was formed in the course of Japan's desperate effort to reconcile tradition and modernity from the Meiji period onwards. The phenomenon of the preservation of the present, on the other hand, can be observed not only in Japan but also in many other late-modern societies around the World. It is interesting to note that these two contrasting undercurrents co-exist today in Japanese cultural heritage management. This is clearly because of the particular history with which the discourse of heritage preservation emerged in the 19th-century and has since been developing in an ever modernised and globalised Japan.

Note

This chapter is a revised and expanded version of my article, 'La logique d'actualisation. Le patrimoine et le Japon', published in the journal *Ethnologie française* in 1995 (http://www.jstor.org/stable/40989704).

References

Aikawa-Faure, N 2014 Excellence and Authenticity: Living National (Human) Treasures in Japan and Korea. *International Journal of Intangible Heritage*, 9: 38–51.

Chiva, I and Levi-Strauss, C 1992 Qu'est-ce qu'un musée des arts et traditions populaires?. *Le Débat*, 70: 165–173.

Douet, J (ed.) 2012 *Industrial Heritage Re-tooled: The TICCIH guide to Industrial Heritage Conservation*. Lancaster: Carnegie.

Eliade, M 1969 *Le Mythe de l'éternel retour*. Paris: Gallimard.

Graburn, N 2008 Multiculturalism, Museums, and Tourism in Japan. In: Graburn, N, Ertl, J and Tierney, R K (eds.) *Multiculturalism in the New Japan: Crossing the Boundaries within*. New York: Berghahn. pp. 218–240.

Hartog, F 2005 Time and Heritage. *Museum International*, 57 (3): 7–18.

Jackson, A and Kidd, J 2011 Introduction. In: Jackson, A. and Kidd, J. (eds.) *Performing Heritage: Research, Practice and Innovation in Museum Theatre and Live Interpretation*. Manchester and New York: Manchester University Press. pp. 1–8.

Nara National Museum 2014. *The Sixty-sixth Annual Exhibition of Shosoin Treasures* (exhibition catalogue). Nara: Nara National Museum.

Ogino, M 1995 La logique d'actualisation. Le patrimoine et le Japon. *Ethnologie française*, 23 (1): 57–64. Stable URL : http://www.jstor.org/stable/40989704

Rousmaniere, N (ed.) 2007 *Crafting Beauty in Modern Japan*. London: British Museum Press.

Tokyo National Museum (ed.) 1973 *Tokyo Kokuritsu Hakubutsukanshi (The History of the Tokyo National Museum)*. Tokyo: Daiichi Hôki.

Evolving and contested cultural heritage in China: the rural heritagescape

Marina Svensson
Lund University

Introduction

Chinese cultural heritage is complex, contested and evolving. There exist different understandings of the content and value of cultural heritage, and a diverse range of manifestations in terms of images, practices and experiences. Today many different actors are involved in debating, mediating, consuming and managing cultural heritage, in contrast with the situation in the past. Chinese

How to cite this book chapter:
Svensson, M 2016 Evolving and contested cultural heritage in China: the rural heritagescape. In: Matsuda, A and Mengoni, L E (eds.) *Reconsidering Cultural Heritage in East Asia*, Pp. 31–46. London: Ubiquity Press. DOI: http://dx.doi.org/10.5334/baz.c.

cultural heritage policy takes place in a historically very unique context, namely an authoritarian/Communist market economy with global aspirations. Negotiations and conflicts over the meaning and management of cultural heritage thus occur in the interface of an authoritarian state, market forces and globalisation. Cultural heritage has become important to the Chinese Communist Party (CCP) in its attempt to foster a cultural and national identity in a society where communism is, if not dead, clearly no longer the powerful cohesive force it used to be. Cultural heritage is therefore central for China domestically in its propaganda and educational work, while at the same time it is used to project China's rising international profile and is a pillar of its soft power strategy. Cultural heritage is also becoming an important economic asset for local governments and tourism related industries, something that opens up potential for new contestations. Increasing wealth and leisure time has led to a rapidly growing middle class and a booming cultural, leisure and tourism industry where different types of heritage experiences are on offer. While cultural heritage has then become important for different regions, cities and local communities in their tourism-related branding strategies, certain groups of people are however unhappy at seeing their cultural practices and heritage sites commodified for the benefit of outside visitors. The processes and contestations surrounding cultural heritage are today highly mediated and visualised, in particular thanks to the impact of the Internet, social media and films, which give a new dimension to the production and consumption of cultural heritage, as well as open up new forums for action and debate.

This chapter is divided into two parts. The first part provides an overview of Chinese cultural heritage policy and practice in order to show the impact of ideology and socio-economic changes on the heritage field. The second part illustrates that impact by focusing on some dramatic changes in rural heritage, in particular vernacular buildings and traditional belief systems and manifestations, and discusses what this implies for local communities. The aim is to show how different factors, such as a crucial ideological shift, rapid economic development and the emergence of a more plural society with new actors, shape and give rise to new visions and contestations related to cultural heritage in the countryside.

Ideology and power in cultural heritage policy and practice: red heritage, patriotism and the logic of the market

Cultural heritage policy touches upon issues of cultural and national identity and is therefore contentious and shaped by power relations (Silverman & Ruggles 2007; Tunbridge & Ashworth 1995). It is important to address and unpack how cultural heritage policy is related to, and shaped by, political and economic power in society. We need to investigate the nature of the cultural heritage that is being protected, whose heritage this is, why it is being protected, how and by whom. Issues of power, agency and social and political capital thus need to be examined, and in this context we particularly need to identify the official discourse and any counter-hegemonic discourses in society.

Smith's concept of an 'authorised heritage discourse' (AHD) is useful for this purpose (Smith 2006). Smith defines AHD as a set of texts and practices dictating the way in which heritage is defined and employed in a given society. While Smith focuses on AHD in Western societies, it is also possible to identify a Chinese AHD, which, although shaped by China's specific political context and development, is also increasingly influenced by international discourses (Svensson 2011; Wang 2010). The designation of something as national heritage tells us what a nation wants to preserve and remember of its past and how it imagines its past. In China's case, the need to make use of cultural heritage for the building of national identity remains strong, but the view of what should be recognised as cultural heritage has undergone significant shifts since 1949.

Generally speaking, we can detect a development over time within the approach to Chinese cultural heritage, from an almost exclusive focus on the revolutionary heritage in the Mao Zedong period, to a focus on China's imperial past and a more culturally based patriotic heritage narrative in the 1980s, to a discovery and celebration of more diverse heritage in the 1990s that also includes vernacular and industrial heritage and finally to the adoption of the concept of intangible cultural heritage since 2000. This development can be traced through studying shifts in ideology and cultural policy that manifest themselves in different heritage and museum policies, sets of heritage listings at the national and local level and in institutional and legislative changes. Regarding physical or 'tangible' cultural heritage, the major actors are the State Administration of Cultural Heritage and the Ministry of Construction, and their equivalents at the provincial, municipal, district and county levels. Regarding intangible cultural heritage, the major actors are the Ministry of Culture and its local offices. But cultural heritage work also involves other institutions and departments, such as government offices responsible for tourism and religious affairs, as well as CCP and its Central Propaganda Department and local offices.

When individuals and groups of people claim or reclaim their identity, or obtain political power, they often challenge or resist the historiography, cultural manifestations and heritage policies of the old political and economic power holders (Harrison 2010). In China, the heritage of so-called 'class enemies', such as capitalists, landlords, lineages and different religious groups, were thus in part destroyed, desecrated and forgotten after 1949. Major historic sites and cultural artefacts were reinterpreted and rewritten through an ideological and political lens and presented as feudal, backward and superstitious, and often only preserved because they could serve as monuments of the 'bad' old days of feudalism, colonialism and capitalism. During the Mao era there was thus an almost exclusive focus on and dominance of revolutionary heritage, such as sites associated with revolutionary events and figures, and collections of revolutionary objects exhibited in new revolutionary museums. The attack and destruction of old cultural artefacts and sites reached a feverish height during the Cultural Revolution. Sites and collections considered of national importance, including the Forbidden Palace, were however spared on orders from the highest leadership.

The new economic policy of the 1980s, however, made CCP turn away from the class struggle and revolutionary rhetoric of the past, and instead engage in re-building legal institutions and restoring social relations that were needed in order to develop the nation's economy. This ideological shift also entailed more tolerance of religious beliefs and cultural practices as well as a re-evaluation of China's past. China's rich cultural heritage now became a source of national pride and much work was put into listing, protecting and restoring hitherto neglected sites and buildings. When we look at lists of heritage sites from the late 1980s onwards, we realise how the proportion of revolutionary sites have diminished, giving way to imperial sites, and how the concept of heritage has also expanded to include vernacular buildings in the countryside, for example ancestral halls and whole villages, as well as industrial sites and more recent buildings. Cultural heritage bureaus have been significantly strengthened and given more financial support, and new museums have been built.

The rapid growth of the number of heritage sites and museums has been impressive. In 1962 the first list of 180 national level protected sites was announced. New rounds of listings have followed at irregular intervals since the early 1980s (1982, 1988, 1996, 2001, 2006 and 2013). Compared with a mere 750 protected sites in 1996, the total number of national sites grew to 4,295 in 2013. While China had only 25 museums in 1949, the number of museums increased exponentially from the 1990s and in particular in recent years. In 2012, 415 new museums opened, making the total number of museums in the country 3,866. In 2006, the first list of intangible heritage included 518 items at the national level, whereas today the number is 1,219. China had its first World Heritage site in 1987 – by 2013 China had 45 World Heritage sites. While the efforts to list heritage sites and build museums have been particularly remarkable since the 1990s, this coincides with the period in which new threats, such as urbanisation, have destroyed much built heritage.

The official Chinese heritage discourse still serves to justify the rule of the Communist Party and its interpretation of history. It is expressed in different policies and laws, and in the selection of protected heritage sites at national, provincial, district and county levels (Svensson 2011). The ideological aspects of cultural heritage are particularly evident in museum work (Denton 2014; Fiskesjö 2010), as well as in the emphasis on patriotic education in schools. While there is still a strong role and place for revolutionary heritage in the Chinese AHD, we also see the emergence of a more culturally based patriotic heritage narrative that celebrates China's imperial history and its artefacts and associated sites. The nationalistic discourse that one can find in so many aspects of contemporary China – for example manifested in the period leading up to and during the Olympic Games in Beijing in 2008 – is also found in the cultural heritage field. This includes calls for repatriation and attempts to buy back artefacts plundered from China during the late Qing Dynasty (Fiskesjö 2010; Kraus 2004).

But the official heritage discourse has also changed and developed due to international co-operation and contacts since the 1980s. Although cultural heritage discourse reflects a given society's history and ideological and political system, international organisations – in particular UNESCO and its work on World Heritage Sites (Hevia 2001; Wang 2010) and Intangible Cultural Heritage (Liang 2013; Obringer 2011) – are increasingly shaping the understanding and management of heritage across the World. In China there is a strong push for and interest in having sites listed as World Heritage and an intense competition among different provinces and regions in this respect. In order to have sites and cultural practices listed, China also has to adopt and fulfil the criteria and management laid down by UNESCO, which brings in new perspectives on cultural heritage.

In the past there was a strong focus on physical or tangible cultural heritage, and many sites were celebrated for their age value, architectural specificities, craftsmanship and grandeur, whereas their cultural or religious significance were often downplayed. Gradually, and under strong influence from UNESCO (Liang 2013; Obringer 2011), China has also started to embrace the concept of intangible heritage (*feiwuzhi wenhua yichan*). China was among the first countries to become a signatory of the UNESCO Convention for the Safeguarding of Intangible Cultural Heritage when it was adopted in 2003. Of 219 items on UNESCO's Representative List of the Intangible Cultural Heritage of Humanity, Chinese entries account for 29. In 2006 China announced its own national level intangible cultural heritage list, and in 2011 a new related law was adopted. This has also led to the establishment of new institutions and a new rhetoric surrounding cultural heritage. However, this way of listing and documenting cultural practices and religious ceremonies should be understood not as a growing tolerance of different cultural and religious practices, but as a new way of managing culture and religion (Liang 2013; Oakes 2013).

New actors and voices in cultural heritage work

In the current political and cultural environment, official cultural heritage discourse and management – manifested through the work and policies of different state bodies such as the State Administration of Cultural Heritage – no longer go unchallenged. In an increasingly plural society with rapidly changing state-society relations, one finds a multitude of actors that celebrate diverse identities, representations of the past and heritage sites. Competing visions of the past and bottom-up struggles to preserve buildings and rituals now also co-exist or compete with the AHD. Since civil society is heavily controlled in China, there are few NGOs in the field of cultural heritage (an example of such an NGO is the Beijing Cultural Heritage Protection Center). Loose networks have however emerged in recent years on the Internet, celebrating heritage in different cities and regions, or specific types of heritage sites or specific cultural practices. There are also vocal intellectuals and journalists who have used the media and various publication formats to raise concerns over the demolition of old urban neighbourhoods and the disappearance of rural heritage (Svensson 2012a).

In the countryside, one should not forget the role played by lineages and religious associations in protecting and renovating ancestral halls and temples. These groups would usually not be recognised as cultural heritage organisations, being fairly loose networks with very little cultural, political and economic power to make their voices heard. The power to define what practices and sites should be elevated to cultural heritage through nominations and listings is tightly controlled by experts, cultural departments and local governments, and there is no open and participatory consultation (Svensson 2011). Nonetheless, lineages and religious associations in rural communities celebrate cultural and religious identities and traditions at local heritage sites or at places that are not always recognised as heritage sites by the state. They also engage in activities that in the past were often dismissed as superstitious and backward but today are increasingly honoured with the term 'intangible cultural heritage'. These historical ironies and the development and implications of the current cultural heritage policy for rural communities will be addressed in the remainder of this chapter.

From feudal buildings and superstitious practices to cultural heritage: the impact of ideological shifts and market forces on the rural heritagescape

The founding of the People's Republic of China drastically changed the economic, cultural and political life in the countryside. Lineages and religious associations were attacked and dissolved as they were seen as a threat to the CCP's political power. Buildings and land belonging to these groups were confiscated, and ancestor and religious worship forbidden or severely restricted. These attacks aimed both at eliminating traditional power elites, and eradicating and appropriating their symbolic and material manifestations. For example, ancestral halls were turned into socialist spaces, and many of them came to serve as schools, cow pens, storage spaces and community centres; ancestral tablets that used to be kept in the halls were removed, traditional carvings were destroyed and placards and writings extolling the virtues of lineages were replaced with revolutionary slogans and portraits of Mao Zedong.

In the 1980s, once the economic reforms had started and the revolutionary rhetoric diminished, many lineages began to reclaim and renovate their ancestral halls, update and compile genealogies and engage in different ancestor ceremonies and ritual festivals. Many lineages also set up small exhibitions about their history in the ancestral halls, including lineage codes and stories of famous ancestors, while also using the halls for ancestor ceremonies and as communal spaces for elderly villagers. They collected money and invested their own labour in this renovation without any support, and often with strong resistance, from local governments. Money was often collected from lineage members living in other places, including abroad, and many small temples were restored with donations from religious believers in the region. For instance, in Zhejiang – where I have conducted fieldwork – ancestor ceremonies and temple fairs in the villages have regained their importance, and as well as serving to create a sense of identity and community, these events strengthen ties with family members who have moved away from the village but who often return for these events.

The official rhetoric has remained highly critical and dismissive of lineages and ancestor ceremonies as examples of 'superstitious, backward and feudal' remnants not fit for a modern civilised peasantry and modern culture, whilst at the same time also worrying about their negative impact on rural governance (Svensson 2012b). Amidst this critique, however, there are also attempts to co-opt and appropriate rural heritage, including lineage history and buildings, as well as temples.

There are two processes at play here, and they are actually intertwined. On the one hand, as briefly mentioned above, since the mid-1990s vernacular cultural heritage in the countryside, including ancestral halls and whole villages, has been 'discovered' and listed as officially protected heritage. On the other hand, tourism, in which cultural heritage constitutes a valuable asset and attraction, has come to be seen as one way for the Chinese countryside to modernize and be lifted out of poverty (Oakes 2013). In 2003, the State Council announced the first list of national level protected historical villages (*lishi wenhua mingcun*). By the end of 2010 there were 169 listed villages. Many provinces have also announced provincial level historic villages. In Zhejiang there are a total of 14 national level historic villages and some 78 provincial level protected historic districts and villages. Two villages in China, Xidi and Hongcun, currently enjoy the status of UNESCO World Heritage sites. The Chinese state's view on religion and minority culture wavers between on the one hand suppression and cautious acceptance of some religious practices and sites, and on the other hand the adoption of such practices and sites within a cultural heritage narrative and tourism agenda (Liang 2013; Oakes 2013; Oakes & Sutton 2010). Rural communities, religious communities and minorities are not passive in this process but are able to take advantage of the cultural heritage discourse and official support for tourism in order to promote their own agenda, identities and beliefs (Oakes & Sutton 2010). Lineages have for example been able to boost their status and position by appropriating the language of cultural heritage and patriotism. Today, therefore, the 'revival' of lineages and rituals as different forces and processes – including market forces, globalisation, official cultural heritage polices, rural tourism projects and development plans – influence how rural communities imagine and create a sense of community and place (Svensson 2012a).

However, when ancestral halls and villages are designated as heritage sites, their use and management often changes, and villages and lineages no longer fully control them. Renovations have to be approved by heritage bureaus and to follow certain guidelines. The official cultural heritage discourse celebrates monumentality, age and aesthetic value over cultural and religious practices associated with these sites. Cultural heritage authorities thus tend to see ancestral halls as cultural relics rather than as living monuments to ancestors. This means that when the halls become heritage sites and tourism attractions, the process of museumification starts, often drastically changing the management and use of these spaces. The original practices of local residents are confronted with those of tourists, giving rise to new patterns of use through 'negotiation' of these spaces, or sometimes to resistance and marginalisation of local communities. The form these processes take inevitably differs from village to village.

In the 1990s, many historical buildings, ancestral halls and old villages were designated as tangible cultural heritage, whereas local cultural practices were still neglected and often dismissed by local governments. Today, however, with the acceptance of the concept of intangible heritage, national and local governments have started to list and manage cultural practices and local rituals. Many cultural traditions and practices, including traditional music and opera, minority music and dances, traditional medicine (Orbinger 2011), traditional handicrafts and religious and ritual practices have made it onto heritage lists that exist at the national, provincial and municipal level. Some of these traditions are seen as threatened and therefore given special protection. For example, the Qiang minorities New Year Festival was inscribed on UNESCO's

Representative List of the Intangible Cultural Heritage of Humanity in need of urgent protection in 2009, since an earthquake in 2008 had destroyed many Qiang villages and put the festival at great risk.

Ancestor ceremonies and temple festivals have in some cases turned into government or tourism sponsored cultural festivals. In one village in Zhejiang, the official promotion of the temple fair downplayed both local lineage and religious associations and marketed the fair as a cultural festival where people could experience rural life and customs in more generic terms. However, it still firmly remains a local affair and villagers return to the village for the ceremony even though tourists and photographers today also crowd the village. In another village in this region, the ancestor ceremonies have been designated as a local level intangible heritage due to the fame of the ancestor.

Both tangible heritage and intangible heritage are seen as important assets that can be marketed for tourism, which is often seen as a way to generate economic growth, lift villages out of poverty and promote modernisation. Tourism has thus been identified as an important tool in the New Socialist Countryside project which aims to modernise the countryside. Rural tourism today includes visits to historic villages, famous temples, scenic areas and so-called *nongjia le*, small peasant restaurants or inns. The new interest in rural tourism can be compared with similar developments in Europe in the late 19th-century, where, as a reaction to urbanisation and rapid social changes, country life and the rural landscape became an object of a 'romantic gaze' and people felt an urgency to preserve and document villages and rural customs that were rapidly vanishing. Similar processes are at play in China today, where the appreciation of picturesque villages and landscapes also feeds into an aesthetic appreciation manifested in traditional art and poetry.

Many local communities, including both Han villages and minority villages, are however experiencing rapid social and economic changes that challenge their sense of place and local identity. Many communities increasingly realise that tourism companies control and market their heritage for tourist consumption. In some places, such as Lijiang, a World Heritage Site, the influx of Han-Chinese businessmen and tourists have radically changed the ethnic make-up and the cultural ambience of the historic quarters (Su 2010, see also Fuquan's chapter in this book).

We have only seen the beginning of a process of museumification or heritagization of the Chinese countryside, although one should remember that much of the countryside is too remote and poor to be of interest to tourists. Many Chinese villages are also facing a serious out-migration that leads to the decrease of younger generations and the sustainability of local culture. Many young people however continue to retain close contacts with their ancestral village through visits during the Chinese New Year, and they invest money in the construction and upkeep of family graves, ancestral halls and temples, as well as contributing to the compilation of new genealogies. There also seems to be a renewed interest in local culture and history among new generations of Chinese people. However, when governments and tour operators elevate villages and their cultural practices to the status of 'heritage', rural life is inevitably changed. As well as bringing new economic possibilities which can enhance but also alter the traditional direction of rural life, the status of 'heritage' also brings new cultural challenges, including the need to cater to visitors who wish to consume an idealised rural life which has little relationship to the reality. The processes of heritagization offer both challenges and opportunities for local communities, as well as giving rise to new questions concerning the importance of place and tradition in a post-Communist world.

References

Chan, S C 2001 Selling the Ancestors' Land: A Hong Kong Lineage Adapts. *Modern China,* 27: 262–284.

Denton, K 2014 *Exhibiting the Past: Historical Memory and the Politics of Museums in Postsocialist China.* Honolulu: University of Hawai'i Press.

Fiskesjö, M 2010 The Politics of Cultural Heritage. In: Lee C K and Hsing, Y (eds.) *Reclaiming Chinese Society: The New Social Activism.* London: Routledge. pp. 225–245.

Harrison, R (ed.) 2010 *Understanding the Politics of Heritage.* Manchester: Manchester University Press.

Hevia, J L 2001 World Heritage, National Culture, and the Restoration of Chengde. *Positions: East Asia Cultures Critique,* 9 (1): 219–243.

Kraus, R 2004 When Legitimacy Resides in Beautiful Objects: Repatriating Beijing's Looted Zodiac Animal Heads. In: Gries P H and Rosen, S (eds.) *State and Society in 21st-century China: Crisis, Contention, and Legitimation.* New York: Curzon. pp. 195–215.

Liang, Y 2013 Turning Gwer Sa La Festival into Intangible Cultural Heritage: State Superscription of Popular Religion in Southwest China. *China: An International Journal,* 11 (2): 58–75

Oakes, T and Sutton, D S (eds.) 2010 *Faiths on Display: Religion, Tourism and the Chinese State.* Lanham, MD: Rowman and Littlefield.

Oakes, T 2013 Heritage as Improvement: Cultural Display and Contested Governance in Rural China. *Modern China,* 39 (4): 380–407.

Obringer, F 2011 Chinese Medicine and the Enticement of Heritage Status. *China Perspectives,* 3: 15–22.

Silverman, H and Ruggles, D F (eds.) 2007 *Cultural Heritage and Human Rights.* New York: Springer.

Smith, L 2006 *Uses of Heritage.* London and New York: Routledge.

Su, X 2010 Heritage Production and Urban Locational Policy in Lijiang. *International Journal of Urban and Regional Research,* 35 (6): 1118–1135.

Svensson, M 2011 Cultural Heritage Protection in the People's Republic of China: Preservation Policies, Institutions, Laws, and Enforcement in Zhejiang. In: Burell, M and Svensson, M (eds.) *Making Law Work: Chinese Laws in Context.* New York: Cornell University Press. pp. 225–266.

Svensson, M 2010 Tourist Itineraries, Spatial Management, and Hidden Temples: The Revival of Religious Sites in a Water Town. In: Oakes, T and Sutton, D S (eds.) *Faiths on Display: Religion and Tourism in China.* Lanham, MD: Rowman and Littlefield. pp. 211–233.

Svensson, M 2012a Heritage Struggles and Place-makings in Zhejiang Province: Local Media, Cross-regional Media Interactions, and Media Strategies from Below. In: Sun W and Chio, J (eds.) *Mapping Media in China: Region, Province and Locality.* London: Routledge. pp. 193–211.

Svensson, M 2012b Lineages and the State in Zhejiang: Negotiating and Re-inventing Local History and Heritage. In: Bislev, A and Thøgersen, S (eds.) *Organizing Rural China.* Lanham, MD: Rowman and Littlefield. pp. 157–172.

Tunbridge, J E and Ashworth, G L 1995 *Dissonant Heritage: the Management of the Past as a Resource in Conflict.* Chichester: John Wiley.

Wang, D 2010 Internationalizing Heritage: UNESCO and China's Longmen Grottoes. *China Information,* 24 (2): 123–147.

The emergence of 'cultural heritage' in modern China: a historical and legal perspective

Guolong Lai
University of Florida

Introduction

In the fall of 1924, the pre-eminent modern Chinese scholar Wang Guowei 王國維 (1877–1927) wrote a long acrimonious letter to Shen Jianshi 沈兼士 (1885–1947) and Ma Heng 馬衡 (1880–1955), directors of the National Beijing University's Department of Chinese Classics (*guoxuemen* 國學門) and its archaeology program. The letter came in response to a 'Manifesto

How to cite this book chapter:
Lai, G 2016 The emergence of 'cultural heritage' in modern China: a historical and legal perspective. In: Matsuda, A and Mengoni, L E (eds.) *Reconsidering Cultural Heritage in East Asia*, Pp. 47–85. London: Ubiquity Press. DOI: http://dx.doi.org/10.5334/baz.d.

for the Preservation of the Ancient Site at Dagongshan' (Baocun Dagongshan guji xuanyan 保存大宮山古蹟宣言) by the University's Archaeological Society, which Wang Guowei had just seen printed in a newspaper (Lui, & Yuan 1984: 405–407; Yuan & Lui 1996: 431–433; see also Bonner 1986: 202–204). The manifesto deplored a Manchu prince's destruction of the 'state property' (*guanchan* 官產) at Dagongshan in the Dajue 大覺 temple, in the western suburbs of Beijing. It went on to accuse the abdicated Last Emperor Puyi 溥儀 (1906–1967), who was still living in the back quarter of the Forbidden City, of having 'taken ancient artefacts (*guqiwu* 古器物) handed down through the ages as his personal property', and called on the Chinese people and the Nationalist government to stop the destruction of national heritage.

Encouraged by another conservative loyalist, Luo Zhenyu 羅振玉 (1866–1940), Wang Guowei argued, against the Manifesto, that the legal status of the site that the Manchu prince had allegedly destroyed was uncertain. More importantly, he asserted that the imperial collections had been historically accumulated by the Manchu emperors, and that:

> 'every object in the imperial palace in addition to those exhibited in the Wenhua and Wuying palaces [in the front part of the Forbidden City], before the Republic compensated the imperial family, under any laws, ancient or modern, Chinese or foreign, is the private property (*sichan* 私產) of the imperial family'.

He continued:

> 'This is also so stipulated in the Republic's own legal document, "*The Articles of Favourable Treatment of the Great Qing Emperor after His Abdication*", which has been under the protection of law and recognized by successive regimes'.

In this letter, Wang declared his resignation from his position at the National Beijing University, severed any connection with the University, and withdrew an article scheduled to be published in the University's journal.

Wang Guowei acutely noted that the real issue at stake was the fate of the imperial collections and the Last Emperor's personal property rights. He was partially right in arguing that in Chinese dynastic history, at least institutionally, the imperial household and the state had distinct budgets and separate finances. Thus, in theory at least, the imperial family's collections and property could be considered as 'private property' under the modern Westernized legal system that the Republic of China had adopted. In fact, as Wang rightfully pointed out, the Republic's '*Articles of Favourable Treatment*' (article 7) guaranteed the Last Emperor's rights in this regard.

However, one could argue, and this seems to have been the opinion of the majority at the time, that the uses and abuses of imperial power often blurred the distinction between the imperial household and the state finances. By insisting on this distinction, Wang took a conservative, legalistic, and somewhat unworldly approach. But for most citizens of the new Republic of China, including many scholars and intellectuals, this distinction had become meaningless. To them, the imperial collections were the essence of the 5,000-year old Chinese civilization, in which the 'spirit of the [Chinese] nation' (*liguo jingshen* 立國精神) reposed (*jituo* 寄托).[1] But why and how could the collections of a fallen Manchu dynasty represent the spirit of a new nation? What other objects and sites could be deemed as 'national heritage'? Why and how did they emerge as national 'cultural heritage'?

In this chapter I try to answer these questions by tracing the evolution of 'cultural heritage' and other related concepts in modern

China from a historical and legal perspective. The Chinese term now used to refer to a nation's or people's heritage from the past, '*wenhua yichan*', 文化遺產, a direct translation of the English term 'cultural heritage', is a neologism that has become popular in Chinese writings only since the 1980s.[2] But similar concepts, such as '*guwu*' 古物 (ancient objects), '*shiji*' 史跡 (historic sites), '*guji*' 古跡 (ancient sites), 'mingsheng' 名勝 (famous sights), '*wenwu*' 文物 (cultural relics), and '*guobao*' 國寶 (national treasures), began to be used right at the inception of modern China, and this was also when the practice of heritage preservation was instituted.

As a national cultural policy, heritage preservation was introduced into China from the West as part of the modernizing efforts under the late Qing dynasty. In fact, the very concept of 'national heritage' emerged with modernity, which in turn compelled the changes in how cultural heritage was conceived and what measures were taken to conserve it. In what follows, I focus on two legislative documents on cultural heritage from the first three decades of the 20th-century. The first document is the '*Measures for the Protection of Ancient Sites* (*Baocun guji tuiguang banfa zhangcheng* 保存古跡推廣辦法章程)' that the Qing government issued in 1909. This is the earliest known Chinese governmental ordinance on the protection of cultural heritage that we know. The second is the '*Law on the Preservation of Ancient Objects* (*Guwu baocun fa* 古物保存法)', issued by the Nationalist government in 1930. These two documents set up the basic legal framework for the protection of cultural heritage in modern China.[3]

Among the different levels of social awareness, the state legislation is the most structured, enduring, and prominent expression of the collective attitude toward the past. By examining the process by which the state's legislative framework came into being, we can see the impact of old practices on heritage preservation in modern China, as well as the introduction of new approaches.

As is well known, the practice of collecting art objects and preserving places with religious or political significance certainly had a long tradition in imperial China. These practices, however, did not lead to a full public and national policy until the end of the 19th-century. Some scholars have argued that, in pre-modern China, precious artefacts, paintings, calligraphic works, bronzes, and so forth, were generally in imperial or private collections; and temples, palaces, and other architectural complexes were in the hands of private owners, religious orders, or the imperial court. These scholars maintain that there was virtually no state ownership of cultural property (see Naquin 2000: xxviii–xxx). Others may disagree. But the modern state stewardship of cultural heritage is often – especially in non-Western developing countries – based firmly on the notion of public ownership. In modern China, as in many other modern nations, the rise of public awareness and the protection of heritage through legislation went along with the building of the modern nation state. Among the art treasures, artefacts, monuments, and sites first declared as 'national heritage' were the imperial collections and property, deserted ancient sites, and archaeologically excavated artefacts.

Educational reform and the introduction of new values

The military and cultural conflicts with the West and Japan in the late 19th-century caused Chinese people collectively to re-evaluate the past. Additionally, by the late 19th-century, China had already embarked, however tentatively and unwillingly, on a new path to modernization and reform, which inevitably undermined traditional ways of valuing the past. The impetus for change emerged from both inside and outside China, but it was the external threats and demands for changes that were to prove to be the more effective catalysts for change.

As a result of the Opium War (1839–1842), the military superiority of the Western powers became the hard truth confronting many Chinese scholars and officials. High officials, such as Zeng Guofan 曾國藩 (1811–1872) and Li Hongzhang 李鴻章 (1823–1901), following their advisors Wei Yuan 魏源 (1794–1856) and Feng Guifen 馮桂芬 (1809–1874), had responded to this revelation by attempting to reform the military and thereby to strengthen China's ability to achieve balance with the West. This includes building arsenals to produce modern weaponry, establishing military schools to train officers, setting up translation schools and institutions to introduce Western knowledge, and sending young students abroad to study military techniques and navigation. The spirit of this so-called 'self-strengthening movement' could be summarized in Zhang Zhidong's (1837–1909) words, 'Chinese learning for essence, Western learning for application' (Zhongxue wei ti, xixue wei yong 中學為體, 西學為用).[4]

However, for a few scholar-officials – such as Guo Songtao 郭嵩燾 (1818–1891), who had been a diplomat in Britain – this 'self-strengthening movement' did not go far enough. These scholars recognized that the weakness of the Qing government and the strength of the Western powers could not be evened out merely by the acquisition of military hardware and technological knowhow; what was necessary, instead, was the reformation of political and social institutions and cultural values (Wang 2006). After China's disastrous defeat in the Sino-Japanese War of 1895, an increasing number of scholar-officials started to call for more thoroughgoing reforms, especially in the political and institutional realms.

Observing the Western practice of the expansion of public institutions in the modernization process, Guo was among the first group of Chinese intellectuals to advocate for the development of public institutions in China; even making an effort to build a public museum (Hu 2000).

Although the Qing court was initially reluctant to change, the Boxer Rebellion in 1900 increased both internal and external pressures, prompting the Empress Dowager Cixi (1835–1908) to issue a reform decree. The policies spelled out therein continued to be implemented throughout the first decade of the 20th-century. This was the Manchu Qing dynasty's final attempt to implement a series of educational, military, and economic reforms in order to modernize China and to strengthen the nation in its military and financial power. Although most of these reforms proved ineffective, they did accelerate the introduction of new social values and the formation of new elites (Wakeman 1975: 228).

In September 1905, the civil service examinations were abolished, and in December, the Ministry of Education was established as the central organ for late Qing educational administration (Guan 2000). The educational reform challenged the role of Confucianism as the state ideology. The Confucian classics had long been used as the basis for written examinations in recruiting young scholars to the administrative service of the imperial state. Even under the new system, the Qing government still attempted to reinforce traditional Confucianism. For example, the regulations concerning educational institutions approved by the Emperor required that on the first and fifteenth days of every month new schools should hold a ceremony of Confucian worship, and the Confucian classics should still be a major part of their curricula (Ichiko 1978). Nevertheless, in reality, Confucianism lost its significance as the state ideology and was no longer the basis of Chinese intellectual life (Schneider 1971).

The educational reforms, the expansion of the public sphere, and the formation of new elites in late imperial China together prepared a platform for the development of new thinking on China's culture and history. New Western ideas and practices were introduced into China through various channels. As early as the 1860s the Qing reformers had opened a school of interpreters in Beijing, where courses on Western sciences and international laws were taught, and where Western books were translated into Chinese. Government-sponsored language schools were soon opened in Shanghai, Guangzhou, Fuzhou, and many other cities. Scholar-reformers such as Kang Youwei 康有爲 (1858–1927), Liang Qichao 梁啟超 (1873–1929), and Yan Fu 嚴復 (1854–1921), who translated the works of Darwin, Huxley, Spencer, and Adam Smith into Chinese, wrote or translated books to promote Western social and political ideas. During his sixteen years of exile after the fiasco of the Hundred-Day Reform in 1898, Kang Youwei visited many museums, ancient ruins, monuments, and archaeological sites all over the World. In the process, Kang developed his own views on how China should preserve its own cultural heritage (Kang 1972). The Qing government also dispatched students and delegations of imperial court officials to study foreign practices in Japan and the West (Spence 1990: 245–246). Among them was the high official and art collector, Duanfang 端方 (1861–1911), who led a group of Qing officials touring the USA, Europe, and Japan from 1905 to 1906 (Lawton 1991: 5–11), during which he visited many world-famous museums. After his return to China, Duanfang proposed to establish public libraries, museums, zoos, and parks (*gongyuan* 公園) as part of the government's ongoing modernization efforts.

An important idea that emerged from these activities was public-mindedness (Qin 2004: 140–142). Anti-Manchu nationalists such as Zhang Binglin 章炳麟 (1868–1936) and Liang Qichao blamed China's weakness on the lack of national or public consciousness. In order to awaken the Chinese people, they urged that new social institutions and social values be advocated. Even the Qing government started to attend to the public needs. Public parks, public museums, and public libraries were introduced into China during this period. In 1906 the imperial delegation brought back from Germany various exotic animals as gifts to the Empress Dowager and put them in the eastern part of the imperial garden in the northwestern suburbs of Beijing. Renamed Wanshengyuan 萬牲園 (the Garden of Ten Thousands Animals), this zoo opened to the public in 1908 as part of the Empress Dowager Cixi's New Policies reforms – the Beijing Zoo is still located in the same place today. The reformer and entrepreneur Zhang Jian 張謇 (1853–1926) suggested to the Qing government that exhibition halls combining the functions of museum and library should be set up. But the government did not heed his suggestion. Zhang eventually established a museum at Nantong in Jiangsu in 1905 (Claypool 2005; Qin 2004: 143–160). This was the first successfully run public museum established by Chinese in China. In the spring of 1909, the Governor of Shandong, Yuan Shuxun 袁樹勛, was permitted by the Qing government to establish a provincial library in Shandong. One of its branches was the 'Shandong Antiquities Preservation Institute (*Shandong jingshi baocunsuo* 山東金石保存所)', the aim of which was to 'collect the old and new unearthed objects and the rubbings [of stone steles and shrine decorations]'. Its collection was put on exhibition and open to the public (Li 1993: 310).

The public consciousness and the process of introduction of new social values continued and was pushed to new levels during the New Culture Movement after the May Fourth movement in 1919, which further introduced new Western ideas such as 'science' and 'democracy'. The introduction of these new ideas and values promoted a re-evaluation of the Chinese past, including the material past (Bao 2000; Guo 2009).

Western exploitation and the public awareness of cultural heritage

In the same period, the plundering of ancient relics by Westerners provoked public and official attention to China's cultural heritage. The best-known cases were the sack of the imperial palaces in Beijing by the Allied Forces of the eight Western powers in 1900,[5] the archaeological expeditions along the Silk Road, the removal of manuscripts from the Dunhuang caves by Aurel Stein (1862–1943) in 1907 and by Paul Pelliot (1878–1945) in 1908 (Hopkirk 1984), and the destruction of Buddhist sculptures at the cave-temple complexes of Tianlongshan, Xiangtangshan, and Longmen. Local warlords also robbed ancient tombs and sold objects to foreign and Chinese collectors. In fact, the majority of the Chinese artworks in Western collections were taken away from China during this period, which was termed by some as a 'Golden Age' for collecting Chinese art objects (Cohen 1992). The awareness that cultural treasures were being stripped from the country at last led to actions to stop it. Among the last ordinances of the moribund Qing, in 1909, was one that explicitly covered protection of cultural sites, namely the already mentioned *Measures for the Protection of Ancient Sites*.[6] Issued by the newly established Ministry of Internal Affairs (*Minzhengbu* 民政部), the *Measures* marked the beginning of a legal framework and of the consciousness of the need to preserve the past from the exigencies of the times.

Although no evidence points to a direct link between the depredations at Dunhuang and the 1909 ordinance, it was certainly not a mere coincidence. Western cultural imperialism in the late 19th- and early 20th-century raised Chinese public awareness of the need to protect the nation's cultural heritage. Although it is often said in Western writings that Stein 'removed' the manuscripts and paintings of the Dunhuang caves, or 'purchased' them from the local Taoist priest Wang Yuanlu (ca. 1849–1931) who was occupying some of the deserted Buddhist caves at the time, recent archival studies of Stein's diaries and documents at the Oxford University library have clearly shown that, during their 'secret transactions', both Stein and Wang were aware of the 'improper' nature of their activities. There is no question that Stein took advantage of the social turmoil in China at that time in order to get these ancient treasures (Wang 2007).

Although strictly speaking the legal status of the Dunhuang caves was not clear, Wang Yuanlu also did not have the right to 'sell' these ancient manuscripts. After the discovery of the library cave by Wang in 1900, local officials ordered that the cave be sealed and these manuscripts and paintings be protected *in situ*. In addition, following the Tang and the Ming legal codes, the Qing dynasty legal code stipulated that, if buried objects (i.e. ownerless property) were found on government or private land, the discoverer could own and use them. The code, however, also stated that if the finds were extraordinary objects (*yichang zhi wu* 異常之物), such as ancient vessels (*guqi* 古器), bells and tripods, talismans and seals that are different from the usual shape (i.e. those objects which should not be possessed in non-government circles [*minjian* 民間]), they should be handed over to the authorities within thirty days; the violators were to be punished with eighty blows with light sticks, and the discovered extraordinary objects were to be placed under government ownership (Tian & Zheng 1999: 266). The Qing government did exactly this after Pelliot's display of some Dunhuang manuscripts in Beijing in 1909. The government ordered local officials at Dunhuang to protect and inventory manuscripts, steles, and sculpture, and commanded that Wang Yuanlu safeguard the manuscripts (Lin, Ning & Luo 1992: 3; Rong 2001: 164–168).

Before his arrival at Beijing, Pelliot visited Duanfang, the then Manchu governor-general of Jiangnan, in Nanjing on June 8, 1909. Duanfang and his associate Miao Quansun (1844–1919) were aware of Pelliot's collection of the Dunhuang manuscripts, but without a clear understanding of the scale of the entire collection in the library cave. Informed of Pelliot's upcoming trip to Beijing, Luo Zhenyu and other Chinese scholars in Beijing approached him. The large scale of Pelliot's collection, the majority of which had already been shipped to France, stunned the Chinese scholars.[7] With Pelliot's permission, Luo and his colleagues copied a list of contents of the documents that Pelliot had sent back; they also photographed eight documents and hand-copied one.[8]

To Chinese scholars, the most important news that Pelliot brought to light was that there were still 8,000 scrolls of manuscripts left in the library cave. Luo Zhenyu reported this to the Ministry of Education, and requested that the Ministry purchase the documents and ship them back to Beijing (Guan 2000: 481–487). On October 2, 1909, five days after Luo had met Pelliot, he sent a letter to the editor of the newspaper *Current Affairs* (*Shiwu bao* 時務報). Luo wrote:

> 'I have heard that there are still manuscripts left in the library cave. I am going to report this to the government authorities and ask them to send a telegraph immediately to Governor-general Mao of Shaanxi and Gansu.

> Although I am not sure whether the remaining documents are still there, if there is any left, I will try my best to push the government [to bring them back]' (Meng 2004).

On the following day, October 3, 1909, the Ministry of Education sent a telegram instructing Governor-general Mao Qingfan to: 'examine the books and documents in the Thousand Buddha's Caves and send them to the Ministry; to examine also the steles and sculptures; and to prohibit the sales of these antiquities to foreigners'.[9] In 1910, the Ministry of Education ordered all the remains of the Dunuang manuscripts to be shipped to Beijing. Although many were lost and stolen in the process, approximately 8,662 scrolls were stored in the Capital Library (now the National Library in Beijing) (Guan 2000: 487). It is interesting to note that when the Ministry of Education ordered the governor of the Gansu Province to protect the Dunhuang materials, the same Ministry also purchased the manuscripts from Wang Yuanlu.[10]

1909 Measures for the Protection of Ancient Sites

It was in the same year, 1909, that the Ministry of Internal Affairs drew up the '*Measures for the Protection of Ancient Sites*'. Established in 1906, the Ministry of Internal Affairs was led by Prince Su Shanqi 善耆 (1866–1922), a prominent figure in late Qing politics. Consistent with routine bureaucratic procedures, the *Measures* were sent to the Emperor as a memorial for review on September 20, 1909. They were published in the *Shibao* 時報 newspaper on October 22, one month after the imperial endorsement.[11] The promulgation of the *Measures* in a widely circulated newspaper showed the interest in the subject on a public level, beyond the government.

The preamble to the *Measures* clearly stated that they were drawn up in reaction to foreigners who had gone inland of China (*neidi* 内地) to buy antiques such as 'ancient steles, stone carvings, paintings and manuscripts, and stone sculptures' to take back to their own countries. It also stated: 'If we permit the outflow [of the antiques], not only is it not agreeable with the spirit of the ancient people, but it also damages the dignity of the nation'. The government's effort was inspired by the fear that China would lose its treasures and dignity as a modern nation in the World. The preamble continued:

> 'In every nation the scope of the items under protection as ancient sites (*guji*) by their ministries of internal affairs is rather large: for examples, the ancient writings (i.e. hieroglyphs) on the Egyptian pyramids, the ancient sculptures of the Greek Temples, the ten-thousand-miles (*li*) long ancient highway of the Romans, and the excavated ancient city of Pompeii'.

The preamble also stated that in these foreign countries:

> 'the old residencies and material remains belonged to the former sages, and some are related to history (*lishi* 歷史), and others are of artistic (*meishu* 美術) significance. No matter large or small, all were collected and treasured'.

The preamble continued:

> '(in these nations) from the imperial household down to the commoners, and from metropolitan centres down to small towns, all have museums to store objects in order to show the achievement of the civilization'.

The *Measures* also made reference to the international laws for the protection of national cultural heritage. They stated that:

> 'as a rule, during military conflicts, other countries cannot destroy [our cultural relics]. Those that have been destroyed in wars should be compensated. This has been written down in international laws (*wanguo gongfa* 萬國公法)'.

The language in the *Measures* matched almost exactly what had been written by the aforementioned entrepreneur Zhang Jian, who proposed that the Qing government establish a national museum: 'There is one great law to protect [the patrimony]. In times of military invasion, the people from other countries cannot take or destroy it. Those who destroy it can be forced to make reparations. This is called international law (*wanguo gongfa*)' (Claypool 2005: 570). The mention of international law in the *Measures* intended, on one hand, to condemn the past lootings by Westerners in China and to prevent further damage by foreign raiding. On the other hand, it reflected the intention to incorporate international law into the Chinese legal system. In 1863, William Alexander Parsons Martin (Chinese name: Ding Weiliang 丁韪良, 1827–1916), an American Presbyterian missionary to China, translated Henry Wheaton's (1785–1848) *Elements of International Law* into Chinese. The translation was commissioned by the Office for the Management of the Business of All Foreign Countries of the Qing central government and was published in 1864 (Wheaton 2000). To include *wanguo gongfa* in the first government legislation for cultural heritage protection, especially the mention of the protection of the enemy's cultural property in time of war, indicates that the Chinese government was aware not only of the recent development in international law but also that it could use it to benefit the interest of China. International agreements in relation to the protection of an enemy's cultural property in time of war appeared in the Hague Conventions of 1899 and 1907, in which the Qing government participated and which it ratified. Furthermore, it shows that the Chinese heritage conservation movement closely followed the international heritage conservation movement from the very beginning.

In addition to the short preamble, the *Measures* included two sections: the first, with six items, focused on the investigation and inventory; the other, with five items, focused on protection. The scope of investigation and inventory included stone carving and petroglyphs, stone sculpture, mural paintings and sculpture, tombs and shrines of the previous dynasties, former sages, famous persons, and excavated objects. These were all the standard items in the writings of traditional local gazetteers. On the one hand, the *Measures* had a strong connection to the traditional practice of antiquarianism that had been practiced in China for over one thousand years. For example, the emphasis was on collecting the rubbings of stone inscriptions, in the formats of naming, recording, and classification of cultural heritage, which all echoed the traditional gazetteer writing. Since the Southern Song dynasty (1127–1279), local officials or social elite had surveyed famous historical and literary figures and the sites associated with them, often from written sources rather than from site visits. The compilation of the lists of these items had become part of the routine of local gazetteer writing and the local practice in protecting cultural sites. In imperial China, as part of central government's administrative control, local officials were obliged to submit to the court an inventory of sites that were protected at the end of each year. Moreover, under the influence of antiquarianism in the Qing dynasty, scholar-official Bi Yuan 畢沅 (1730–1797), the then governor of Shaanxi, in 1776 compiled an illustrated list of the historical sites of Shaanxi, *Guanzhong shengji tuzhi* 關中勝跡圖誌.

In this work, Bi Yuan established a set of measures to protect ancient sites: demarcating the boundaries (the four corners), erecting boundary stones and walls, leaving latitude (*yudi* 餘地) in the outside of the walls (a 'buffer zone'), and designating personnel to manage the sites.

This type of social survey was the very technique that a modern national government used to collect objective and systematic information for governing (Lam 2011). In fact, the *Measures* specifically required local officials to go to the field to investigate, rather than submitting the old yearly bureaucratic memorandum. Another way in which the *Measures* went beyond the traditional practice was its expanded categories of protected sites. The *Measures* were specifically targeted at objects, monuments, and sites that related to the commoner, going beyond the usual categories of imperial mausoleums, ancient tombs (*guxi lingqin* 古昔陵寢), and temples and burials of former sages (*xianxian cimu* 先賢祠墓) which often appeared in the local and national gazetteers. Such departure from the old gazetteer surveys of ancient sites was very much influenced by foreign models. It is significant that the word '*guji*' instead of more common word '*guwu*' was used here, because during this period '*guwu*' often referred to both movable objects and monuments and sites.

In summary, the 1909 Measures for the Protection of Ancient Sites not only connected to the traditional practice of valuing art collections as well as imperial and religious sites, but also set up the framework for the protection of public monuments and art collections (in contrast to the 'private' collections of the emperors and members of the elite). It recognized two of the three categories of values that have been often ascribed to cultural heritage in modern China: historic and artistic values (the third one being scientific).

The second section of the *Measures* included specifications about relocating stone objects, establishing regulations for the making of rubbings from steles, and erecting signs in front of important tombs and shrines. One of the most significant concepts mentioned in the *Measures* was the protection of mural paintings and sculptures. The relevant part stated:

> 'The exquisite mural paintings and sculptures should be protected. No damage is allowed. No repainting is allowed on those blurred images, in order not to lose the original appearance (*benlai mianmu* 本來面目). Otherwise [if it is repainted], we would see nothing of the ancient fine art'.

This was quite a departure from the traditional way of preserving religious images, which often repainted blurred images afresh. Another important reason for establishing public museums at the provincial level was that they could become public institutions for accepting donations, displaying art treasures, and educating the people. On this the *Measures* stated: 'if treasures cannot be appreciated by everyone, how can we ask everyone to love and care for them in case of unfortunate events?' Thus, 'every provincial capital should establish a museum to collect, to categorize, and to store [art treasures]', so that those who wanted to donate could donate, and those who wanted to temporarily store their treasures could do so too. The *Measures* continued: '(t)hus all treasures in the world can be shared by everyone. This not only can avoid the harmfulness of the seclusion, but also obtain the benefit of preservation'. Although it is still uncertain where these new ideas came from, and how and by whom they were incorporated into this document, it is clear that the 1909 ordinance marked a new beginning in the national protection of cultural heritage.

Public ownership and the fate of the imperial property

The Qing dynasty ended in 1911 with the abdication of the Last Emperor Puyi. This event would profoundly affect the consideration of what constituted 'the past', and one started seeing the transformation of private and imperial places and spaces into public ones – state legislation played an important role in this process.

The presidency of the newly founded Republic went from Sun Yat-sen (1866–1925) to Yuan Shikai (1859–1916), a former Qing military official, who negotiated for the Qing abdication and controlled the imperial army. Under the arrangements of the *Articles of Favourable Treatment of the Great Qing Emperor after His Abdication*, the Last Emperor and his close associates continued residing in the rear part of the Forbidden City until 1924, when the Last Emperor was expelled from it by the General Feng Yuxiang 馮玉祥 (1882–1948). As mentioned at the beginning of this chapter, the fate of the imperial property and collections was debated before and during this period.

Still living in the Forbidden City, the young Emperor Puyi held his title and was surrounded by the imperial household and a group of loyalists, some of them casting greedy eyes on the imperial collections still housed in the imperial residence. But with the imperial dynasty gone, places such as the Temple of Heaven and the Altar of Earth and Grain, in the suburbs of Beijing, became overgrown with weeds and littered with refuse; although the Summer Palaces in the west suburbs and the imperial ancestral temples within the Forbidden City remained well preserved. How the neglected properties should be managed, and who had the right to own and dispose of them, were hot issues among not only members of the imperial household and the Qing loyalists but also the officials of the new Republican government as well as scholars and the common people. In November 1914, the Institute for Exhibiting Antiquities (*Guwu chenlie suo* 古物陳列所) in the Wenhuadian and Wuyingdian Halls in the front part of the Forbidden City opened its gate to the public. The Institute was set up by the Ministry of Internal Affairs, under the leadership of Zhu Qiqian 朱啓鈐 (1872–1964), to take over the ancient relics in the imperial collections that were housed outside of Beijing, from Fengtian (i.e. Shenyang), the homeland of the Qing, and the imperial summer resort at Jehol (Chengde) (Hang 2005; Wang 2010).

As shown at the beginning of this chapter, to Wang Guowei – who had become ultraconservative politically and served as the Emperor's Companion of the Southern Study – the controversies and disputes over the imperial treasures were more than just an issue of property rights. Wang was assisting in inventorying the palace treasures such as books, bronzes, porcelains, jades, and paintings at the time. In his aforementioned letter to Shen Jianshi and Ma Heng and the Archaeological Society at Beijing University, Wang went further to accuse his colleagues at the university of being unwise and unkind and lacking in courage:

> 'Not to study either the history of the palace collections or the *Articles of Favourable Treatment* is unwise. To be familiar with both and yet deliberately to say this is unkind. The Archaeological Society was against the Ministry of Internal Affairs' "Opinions on the draft of the laws on protection of ancient books, objects, and sites", but did not make any criticism of the Republican authority's illegal takeover of the ancient relics from the imperial family to establish the Institute for Exhibiting Antiquities; instead the Society slanders the imperial family; being as it is a case of "devouring the weak and spitting out the strong" is uncourageous' (Yuan & Liu 1996: 432).

Wang complained that by adopting the position as indicated in the manifesto, his colleagues at Beijing University ignored not only their legal duty as citizens of the Republic of China but also their sacred duty as independent scholars and their moral obligations as human beings. He continued:

> 'If you are still a national university founded by the Republic of China, it is most certainly your duty to comply with the *Articles* by which the Republic was created as well as with its laws regarding the protection of private property. Universities are the highest institutions of learning in the entire country, and you gentlemen also uphold scholarship as your responsibility. When you make statements, therefore, you ought not to speak carelessly. Scholarship is certainly one of the highest enterprises of the human race, but if it is conducted without the support of moral and legal principles, it surely cannot stand alone. To protect ancient objects is only one goal of scholarship, but if, for the sake of preserving antiquities, one violates fundamental rights recognized in both laws and morality, both state and society will disintegrate and where will scholarship be then?' (Yuan & Liu 1996: 433)

As stated earlier, Wang forthwith severed all relationships with Beijing University.

Earlier on, on May 18, 1924, sensing the mounting political pressure, Wang Guowei had submitted a proposal to the young Emperor to use the imperial collections as a shield to protect the imperial family. In this proposal he suggested that a section of the Forbidden City should be opened as a Museum of the Imperial Household:

> 'Now I have a plan, which has the advantage of protecting the imperial family but is without any harm. I suggest

> that a part of the Forbidden City should be opened as a Museum of the Imperial Household, displaying the ancient vessels and calligraphies and paintings from the Imperial Household; let all the people, Chinese and foreign, have the opportunity to appreciate them.... Thus the Forbidden City will become a gathering-place of Chinese culture, and will also forge an important connection to the world cultures. In case these are military affairs in the Capital, all the counties will have the responsibility to protect it' (Yuan & Liu 1996: 416–417).

Wang Guowei's suggestion certainly did not attract the attention of the young Emperor. Five months later, the Last Emperor was expelled from the Forbidden City, and the palace treasures, except for those that the Last Emperor smuggled out, were inventoried by the Committee on Affairs Related to the Qing Imperial Family, and became the bulk of the collections of the Palace Museum, opened to the public on October 10, 1925.

Meanwhile, other public museums opened. One such museum was the Institute for Exhibiting Antiquities, led by Zhu Qiqian, an important figure in the modernization of Beijing and the protection of its cultural heritage during the early Republican period. After spending his childhood with his diplomat stepfather in France, Zhu came back to China as a young man, and launched an official career, highly trusted by the presidents Yuan Shikai and Xu Shichang (1855–1939). Soon he became a powerful figure in the Beiyang government. Zhu served as the Minister of Internal Affairs and the president of the Municipal Council. He travelled frequently to Japan, France, England, and the USA, and was familiar with the Western-style municipal administration. He attempted to apply what he learned to the modern transformation of the city. He was also a strong advocate of building and renovating the capital's streets, gates, sewage system, and public transport. In June 1914, he initiated the establishment of the Municipal Council of Beijing (*Jingdu shizheng gongsuo* 京都市政公所). Under his leadership, a public park was created in the deserted imperial Altar of Earth and Grain near the Tian'anmen in 1914.[12] Zhu was also interested in traditional Chinese craftsmanship. In 1919 he discovered a Song dynasty copy of the architectural manual *Yingzao fashi* (營造法式); he collated it with different editions, and finally published the result in 1923.

One of Zhu's achievements in regard to the protection of cultural heritage was the promotion of technological development and the scientific uses of the past. In December 1913, the Ministry of Internal Affairs (*neiwubu* 內務部) issued the 'The Bylaws of the Institute for Exhibiting Antiquities' (*Guwu chenliesuo zhangcheng* 古物陳列所章程).[13] In the preamble to these bylaws, Zhu Qiqian set forth the motivation for establishing the Institute:

> 'Those who study the ancient subjects use them [i.e. *guwu*, ancient relics] to discover theories and natural laws, to observe the process of natural evolution, to explore the ingenuity of creation and production, and to examine the historical changes in human affairs. All the countries in the East and West collected treasures and establish special institutions in order to show the prosperity of production and to promote the study of fine arts. They pay special attention to the protection of ancient objects, and endeavour to guard them without loss'.

This apparently was a great departure from the traditional antiquarian goal, using antiquities to verify the ancient historiography and to legitimize political power. Here the preservation of cultural heritage was not for personal pleasure but for social progress and the public good. The function of museums as educational organizations was considered to display technological advancement. This way of valuing the past was very different from the traditional ones. Zhu's approaches had been influenced by the ideas of progress and Darwinism, as well as industrial expositions in other parts of the World in the late 19th- and early 20th-century, in which technology, industrial production, and its products were emphasized.

Zhu Qiqian further stated that since individual scholars did not have enough resources to guard the nation's cultural treasures, it became the government's responsibility to collect and protect ancient objects. Thus, the first article in the bylaws stated that: 'the Institute for Exhibiting Antiquities is in charge of the preservation of ancient relics and was subordinated by the Ministry of Internal Affairs'. At the same time, the Committee for Promoting the Protection of Ancient Relics was established and affiliated with the Institute. Another important point in this document was the issues related to the ownership of the cultural heritage. Against the background of the government's attempt to restrict the sales of ancient antiquity to foreigners, the bylaws emphasized the public ownership of cultural property. Reflecting the vast foreign trade of Chinese antiquities during this period, the consideration of moveable objects was given most emphasis (see Cohen 1992).

Nationalism and the scientific value of archaeological heritage

The establishment of the Institute for Exhibiting Antiquities and the Palace Museum concluded the fate of the Qing imperial art collections and property. Except for those art objects taken by the Last Emperor and others – the majority of which ended up in

Western museums – the imperial collections and property now belonged to the nation. However, the opening of art markets in the West and Japan for Chinese antiquities had taken a terrible toll on China's archaeological heritage. The most appalling incident was the warlord Sun Dianying's (1889–1947) rifling of the tombs of Emperor Qianlong and Empress Dowager Cixi in the Eastern Mausoleums near Zhunhua, Hebei province in May 1928.

After reuniting China and moving its capital from Beijing to Nanjing in 1927, the Nationalist government, led by General Chiang Kai-shek (1887–1975), started vehement nation-building campaigns. The surge of nationalism and the interplay with academic politics prompted scholar-politicians such as Fu Sinian 傅斯年 (1896–1950) to use new, Western, scientific archaeology to fight with both regionalism and imperialism (Lai 1999). The Chinese government started to exert tighter control on foreign expeditions and on the removal of antiquities from China, and the legislation on cultural heritage developed. Governmental and private institutions were established to take care of the cultural heritage. One of Fu's weapons was the national legislation on the protection of cultural heritage. In 1930, under the promotion of Fu Sinian, Li Ji 李濟 (1896–1979), and Dong Zuobin 董作賓 (1895–1963), the Nationalist government issued the 'Law on the Preservation of Ancient Objects' (*Guwu baocun fa* 古物保存法) (Li 1996: 87–90), which clearly articulated the state ownership of all archaeological artefacts, and established a registration system for the control of private collections and limited the circulation and antiques trade. This state ownership included the right of excavation and the right to grant excavation licenses. The 1930 law set up the basic framework for protecting archaeological heritage that is still at work in the People's Republic today.

1930 Law on the Preservation of Ancient Objects

From a historical point of view, as Wang Guowei remarked in relation to the legal status of the imperial collections, in China the right to hold property of underground archaeological heritage traditionally privileged land owners and finders. Since the Tang legal code (in *Tanglü shuyi*), which was subsequently adopted by the Ming and Qing legal codes, the objects excavated by the land owners on their own property had belonged to themselves. When objects were discovered in other people's property, the finder should split half of the value with the property owner. The 1930 Law on the Preservation of Ancient Objects radically changed this centuries-long practice. As Articles 2 and 7 state, all underground artifacts now came to belong to the state (Li 2013: 110–126):

> 'Article 2: For all ancient relics, except for those privately owned, the Central Committee on Protection of Ancient Relics (*Zhongyang guwu baoguan weiyuanhui* 中央古物保存委員會, abbreviated as CCPAR) assigns an appropriate location and institution for protection.'

> 'Article 7: All ancient objects underground or exposed on the surface belong to the nation. When such objects are discovered, the discoverer bears the responsibility to report to the local administrative office, which then reports to the higher authorities. Under the guidance of the Ministry of Education, the Ministry of Internal Affairs, and the CCPAR, the discovered relics should be received and protected. The discoverer should be rewarded properly. Discovering without reporting, as well as attempting to hide ancient objects, will be treated as theft.'

Another feature of the 1930 law was a new, scientific definition of '*guwu*':

> 'Article 1: 'the term *guwu* in this law refers to all the ancient objects related to archaeology, history, paleontology, and other branches of scientific studies. The Central Committee on the Protection of Ancient Relics (CCPAR) defines the scope and category of *guwu*'.

The law also creates a new national organization in charge of ancient relics, the CCPAR.

> 'Article 9: the CCPAR consists of 6 to 11 experts appointed by the State Council (*xingzhengyuan*), 2 representatives from the Ministry of Education and the Ministry of Internal Affairs, and a representative from each national museum'.

The law also established a registration system for the control of private collections (Articles 5 and 6) and limits the circulation and antiquity trade (Articles 6 and 13).

Furthermore, the state ownership came to include the right of excavation as well as the right to grant license for excavation:

> 'Article 8: the excavation of ancient relics should be conducted by academic institutions under the central or local government. The excavation project must be approved by the CCPAR, and licensed by the Ministry of Education and the Ministry of Internal Affairs. Those excavations without appropriate license are treated as thievery'.

> 'Article 10: If it is necessary for foreign academic institutions or experts to participate in the excavation, it should be approved by the CCPAR'.

Following this law, several supplementary regulations were issued: the so-called 'detailed regulations' (古物保存法施行細則1931); the regulations on the organization of the CCPAR

(中央古物保存委員會組織條例1932); the regulations on excavation of ancient relics (採掘古物規則1935); the regulations on the participation of foreign institutions or individuals in excavation (外國學術團體或私人參加掘採古物規則1935); and the regulations on certification for export of ancient relics (古物出國護照規則1935).

The significance of the 1930 law and related regulations lay in its pioneering role in establishing a new scientific definition of '*guwu*', which connected the objects of the past directly to modern disciplines introduced from the West. This scientific approach to physical remains of the past was reflected in the new ways of collecting data, the emphasis on archaeological fieldwork, and the insistence on the recording of the context where the objects were found, instead of just seeking treasure. The establishment of a national committee on cultural heritage institutionalized the control of cultural heritage.

The background of the 1930 Law on the Preservation of Ancient Objects was the Yinxu excavation, which the newly established Institute of History and Philology of the Academia Sinica had been conducting from 1928 in Anyang, Henan Province, the site of the last capital of China's earliest dynasty, the Shang. Under the leadership of Fu Sinian and Li Ji, this excavation was in the beginning an international cooperation with the Freer Galley of Art in Washington DC. The excavations were, however, interrupted several times. The initial agreement between the Institute of History and Philology and the local warlord Feng Yuxiang who controlled Henan at the time, was established thanks to Feng's submission to the Nationalist government. In May of 1929, however, the soldiers protecting the staff of the Yinxu project suddenly withdrew from the site, as Feng Yuxiang had defied Chiang Kai-shek's ban on the assembling of local armies and now began a war against the central Nationalist government.

Under the circumstances, Li Ji's decision to ship some of the artefacts to Beijing seems very reasonable. Nevertheless, he was promptly accused by local people and the provincial authorities of violating the agreement reached between the Henan government and the Institute of History and Philology. The original provincial permission had no mention of this issue. Only later had He Rizhang 何日章 (1893–1979), director of the Henan Provincial Library (Dashan 2007), suggested to the provincial government that the Yinxu treasures should be exhibited in Kaifeng, the provincial capital. The local authority quickly endorsed his suggestion. When this request reached the institute, it provoked a vague response – the issue of ownership was negotiable; after all, the institute was devoted to research, not to the acquisition of artefacts.

In October 1929, He Rizhang informed Li Ji that the Henan authorities had decided to prohibit all digging at Yinxu by the Institute of History and Philology – the process of excavating the site was soon taken over by the Henan Museum of Ethnography.[14] Both parties to the dispute timed their moves in accordance with the vicissitudes of the conflict between Chiang Kai-shek and Feng Yuxiang, and those who held the right to excavate Yinxu were those who held political sway.

Fu Sinian immediately began looking for ways to settle the dispute through political channels. He contacted Wu Zhihui 吳稚暉 (1865–1953), a senior member of the Nationalist party who had regular contact with Chiang Kai-shek. Through this trusted official, Chiang Kai-shek became convinced of the importance of compelling the Henan local government to cooperate with the

Institute's project. Fu Sinian, Li Ji, and Dong Zuobin also campaigned for the national legislation on archaeological heritage. The result was the 1930 Law on the Preservation of Ancient Objects. Furthermore, in order to convince local people to see the Yinxu excavation as a national event, Fu Sinian lectured on the use of archaeological discoveries in reconstructing national history. However, the Institute of History and Philology did not resume the work at Yinxu until Feng Yuxiang's war was concluded and Chiang Kai-shek regained control over Henan.

On the international level, the issue of ownership of archaeological heritage was also the incentive to agreement and dispute. Although not explicitly stated, one of the Freer Gallery's goals for archaeological excavations in China was certainly to get new data and possibly objects from secure archaeological contexts. As associate curator of the Freer from 1922 to 1934, Carl W. Bishop (1881–1942) led several archaeological expeditions in China. In the late 1920s, Bishop invited Li Ji, who had just returned from Harvard after obtaining a Ph.D. degree in anthropology, to participate in archaeological cooperation. Li Ji was sensitive to the issues of Western exploitation of Chinese cultural relics. He asked Bishop about the ownership of artefacts excavated in China, to which Bishop responded rather patronizingly:

> 'Your touching upon the subject of removal of art objects from Chinese soil opens up a very large and important subject, with the most far reaching ramifications, and especially thorny through the vested interests – art dealers both Chinese and foreign – concerned. I have some very decided ideas in this regard, however – ideas which I feel pretty sure will meet with your warm approval and support. I have not yet thought these out to the point where I can put them adequately upon paper; but it seems to me that I am slowly working toward a solution

> that will be fair to all. The time was when the notion of the Powers returning any portion of the Boxer Indemnity funds would have been laughed at; yet the needed change of feeling has been brought about, and it has always given me the sincerest pleasure to know that the United States took a leading part in initiating this movement.
>
> There are several possibilities concerning the future treatment of Chinese art objects. I believe a beginning has already been made in the return of these to Chinese possession. Here, doubtless, the question of ownership, both original and actual, would come up. Another possibility is that of sending abroad loan collections, to be exhibited in certain definite foreign institutions for a period of years. It is unfortunately too true that the real greatness of China – her achievements in the past and her vast potentialities for the future – have been obscured during the past few years by news of bandits, floods, famines, and civil disorder to an extent wholly beyond the facts. No nation to – day can live to itself alone; and I for one should like nothing better than to give all the aid in my power in the direction of placing China in a proper light, particularly before the people of the United States.'[15]

Bishop stated that his mission was to reveal 'the real greatness of China' to the people of the United States, to advance 'true scientific research', and to bring about 'the best possible understanding between the peoples'. He assured Li Ji that 'you would be asked to do nothing which you might feel incompatible with your allegiance to the Republic of China'.[16]

Li Ji was satisfied with the answer, although he did not miss the vagueness of Bishop's response. With the rise of nationalist sentiment in China, the possibility of setting up a mutually beneficial cooperation disappeared. The Freer Gallery of Art withdrew from the Yinxu excavation in 1930. The vagueness in the original agreement between the gallery and Li Ji gave rise to a series of disputes over the purpose of the excavation and the treatment of the unearthed artefacts (Li 1996: 62–65). In a situation that mirrored the conflicts at Yinxu of nationalism versus localism, national archaeology had to do battle with imperialist greed. It is in the context of dealing with both regionalism and foreign imperialism on the ownership of Chinese antiquities that the 1930 law was legislated.

Conclusion

In this chapter, I have traced the process of the transformation of cultural property from imperial and mostly private possessions in late imperial China to public monuments and state-owned cultural heritage of the early Republic through the use of state legislations and administrative orders. Attempts at modernization in China were evident toward the end of the Qing dynasty, but they were feeble and had only a marginal impact on the physical protection of cultural heritage. After the abolishment of the old civil examination system, education reforms started in order to face the challenge of the West and to modernize the old society. New social institutions such as public museums and libraries and new social values were introduced. During a temporary break from tradition, most imperial monuments were ignored and abandoned. Facing the challenge of the Western powers, the older Confucian ideology declined, and a new modern Western-influenced state ideology was developed. The central government and social elites took a new look at China's cultural heritage. In 1909, the Qing government ordered the protection of ancient objects and monuments, and later ordered a national survey of existing ancient objects and monuments.

In the meantime, Westerners' explorations and stealing of ancient relics from China had provoked Chinese scholars, the public, and the government to pay attention to their cultural heritage. Several officials suggested establishing museums in China. Under Zhu Qiqian's leadership, the Institute for Exhibiting Antiquities was set up in 1914; the imperial palace in Beijing finally opened to the public in 1925, and the National Museum of History opened in 1926. With the introduction of new disciplines from the West, such as modern history, archaeology, anthropology, and architectural history, the old cultural heritage acquired new scientific values and meaning.

It is important to note that Chinese conservation movements have been mainly promoted by the nation-state. The control of cultural heritage in modern China is viewed as part of the state sovereignty – it is a political issue first and foremost. In the first half of the last century, the need to maintain sovereignty was closely linked to the claim of state ownership of cultural heritage and to the efforts to prevent foreigners from stealing and exporting ancient relics overseas.

Although very different in its political ideology from the Nationalist government, the Communist government after 1949 adopted the basic system set up by the 1930 Law on the Preservation of Ancient Objects. The current legal framework is basically an elaboration of this old system. This legal framework is quite defensive (emphasizing state ownership), prescriptive, and conservative. It stresses the issue of ownership and control, and is far less clear about issues of management. Today, Chinese heritage conservation is in the midst of a historical change, a dramatic shift from a state-monopolized enterprise to a multiple-channelled social project that will proceed at three levels: the national, the local, and the international. This transition has presented many difficult issues and challenges, but at the same time, it also provides opportunities and hope.

Notes

[1] Cited from a telegram, dated 12 November 1923, in which the Educational Society of Hubei Province urged the Beijing government to stop the Qing imperial family from selling ancient artefacts: see Li 2013: 36–37.

[2] The term 'heritage' was first institutionalized in the West in Britain in 1975: see Pai 2013: xv–xvi.

[3] This legal framework was basically followed even after the Communists took over China in 1949, such as in the 1982 Cultural Relics Law. Not until recently – in the revision of the Cultural Relics Law in 2002 – did things begin to change, especially in terms of the relaxed regulation on the domestic art markets and the emphasis on the economic value of cultural heritage.

[4] For the 'self-strengthening movement', see Spence 1990: 216–224 and Kuo & Liu 1978: 491–542.

[5] After the International Expedition crushed the Boxer Uprising and occupied Beijing, looting by Western troops began and was soon out of control. Wilbur J. Chamberlin (1866–1901) recorded the extraordinary scale of looting. See Chamberlin 1904, especially pages 100–107.

[6] *Da Qing fagui daquan* 大清法規大全 (The complete law and regulation of the Great Qing). 1972, Reprint 1910 Shanghai Zhengxueshe edition, Taipei: Hongye shuju, Minzhengbu, vol. 2; juan 15, 'Baocun guji'.

[7] For Pelliot's trip to Beijing, see Jiqing 2011.

[8] Luo Zhengyu's *Dunhuang shishi yishu* 敦煌石室遺書 (The remaining documents from Dunhuang's Cave Library) and *Liusha fanggu ji* 流沙訪古記 (Visiting antiquity in the shifting sands) were both published at the end of 1909.

[9] 'Xing Shan Gan zongdu qing chi chayan jianxi Qianfodong shuji jiebu bing zaoxiang gubei wu ling wairen goumai dian 行陝甘總督請飭查驗檢析千佛洞書籍解部並造像古碑無

令外人購買電', *Xuebu Guanbao* 學部官報 (Ministry of Education Bulletin), October 1909, no. 104.

10 Luo Zhenyu proposed that the Ministry of Education should buy the Dunhuang manuscripts, while others suggested that the Ministry could use its administrative power to seize the manuscripts. Luo Zhenyu insisted that because the Gansu province was poor, the Ministry should pay to obtain them. In the end, the Ministry paid 6000 liang of silver, but this money was embezzled by local officials and Wang Yuanlu only got 300 liang of silver, less than what he had received from Pelliot. In 1907, Stein paid about 200 liang of silver to Wang Yuanlu and took away 29 boxes of manuscripts. In 1908, Pelliot paid 500 liang of silver. See Xinjiang 2001: 167–168. For what exactly Stein paid Wang and how many manuscripts and paintings he obtained, see Wang 2007.

11 *Shibao*, XT 1/9/9 (Oct. 22/1910), p. 5.

12 It was first called '*Zhongyang gongyuan*' (Central Park), and changed to '*Zhongshan gongyuan*', named after Sun Yat-sen in 1928. Other parks include Beihai Park (North Sea) in the old Imperial city opened in 1925; the Altar of Heaven in 1918; the Jingzhao Park, based on Earth Altar (Ming) outside north city wall, in 1925 (years of neglect and abuse by soldiers stationed nearby had turned it into wasteland); and the South City Park (near the Altar of Agriculture; not associated with the cultural monument) in 1917. Summer Palace and residential quarters of the Forbidden City were added to the 'list of public spaces' in 1924. As the head of Beijing's Central Park Administration, Zhu Qiqian ruled that no buildings in the park could be demolished or renovated without its approval; the same rule applied to other parks later; but new buildings, new plantings, and new uses of the place were allowed (ergo, no attempt to maintain the integrity of the parks as historic places). What Zhu Qiqian did in the Central Park was, first, to preserve all the important imperial ritual structures of the Ming and Qing dynasties under the protection of the state; second, to protect the old trees in the park; third, to relocate several pillars and steles from the ruins

of Yuanming yuan to the Central Park and to install the stone lions from the Song dynasty discovered near Beijing; fourth, to build new facilities to accommodate the function of this place as a public park, for example, public toilets and benches; and fifth to plant trees and flowers. See Shi 1998: 233–236.

[13] In 1948 the Institute for Exhibiting Antiquities merged with the Palace Museum.

[14] Under Feng Yuxiang's sponsorship, the Henan Provincial Museum was established in 1927. In May 1928, its name changed to 'Museum of Ethnography' in order to propagate 'the ideal of national and universal harmony'. In December 1930, it changed its name back to Henan Provincial Museum.

[15] Carl Whiting Bishop Correspondence, dated March 23, 1925, in the Freer Gallery of Art records, Li Chi file, housed in the Smithsonian Institution Archives, Washington DC.

[16] *Ibid.*

References

Bao X 鮑小會 2000 Zhongguo xiandai wenwu baohu yishi de xingcheng 中國現代文物保護意識的形成. *Wenbo,* 文博 3: 75–80.

Bi Y 畢沅 (1730–1797) 2004 Zhang P 張沛 (ed.) *Guanzhong shengji tuzhi*關中勝跡圖誌. Xi'an: San Qin chubanshe.

Bonner, J 1986 *Wang Kuo-wei: An Intellectual Biography.* Cambridge. MA: Harvard University Press.

Chamberlin, W J 1904 *Ordered to China, Letters Written from China While under Commission from the New York Sun during the Boxer Uprising and the International Complications which Followed.* London: Methuen.

Claypool, L 2005 Zhang Jian and China's First Museum. *Journal of Asian Studies,* 64 (3): 567–604.

Cohen, W I 1992 *East Asian Art and Culture: A Study in International Relations.* New York: Columbia University Press.

Guan X 關曉紅 2000 *Wan Qing xuebu yanjiu* 晚清學部研究. Guangzhou: Guangdong jiaoyu chubanshe.

Guo X 郭璇 2009 Chengchuan yu jiaorong: Xifang wenming dui Zhongguo jindai wenhua yichan baohu de yingxiang 承傳與交融: 西方文明對中國近代文化遺產保護的影響. *Xin jianzhu* 新建築, 6: 73–76

Hang X 杭曉春 2005 Huihua ziyuan: you "micang" zouxiang "kaifang" 繪畫資源: 由'秘藏'走向'開放. *Wenyi yanjiu* 文藝研究, 2: 118–127.

Hopkirk, P 1984 *Foreign Devils on the Silk Road: The Search for the Lost Cities and Treasures of Chinese Central Asia*. Amherst: University of Massachusetts Press.

Hu C 胡長明 2000 Guo Songtao dui xifang shehui gongyi wenhua shiye de kaocha 郭嵩燾對西方社會公益文化事業的考察. In: Wang X 王曉天and Xu Y 胥亞 (eds.) *Guo Songtao yu jindai Zhongguo duiwai kaifang* 郭嵩燾與近代中國對外開放. Changsha: Yuelu shushe.

Ichiko, C 1978 Political and institutional reform, 1901–1911. In Fairbank, J K (ed.) *The Cambridge History of China*, vol. 10, Late Ch'ing, 1800–1911. Cambridge: Cambridge University Press. pp. 376–383.

Kang Y 康有爲 1972 Baocun Zhongguo mingji guqi shuo 保存中國名跡古器說. In: Kang W 康文佩 (ed.) *Kang Nanhai (Youwei) xiansheng nianpu xubian* 康南海有爲先生年譜續編. Taipei: Wenhai chubanshe. pp. 95–106.

Kuo, Ti-Y, and Liu, K-C 1978 Self-strengthening: the pursuit of Western technology. In: Fairbank, J. K. (ed.) *The Cambridge History of China,* vol. 10, Late Ch'ing, 1800–1911. Cambridge: Cambridge University Press. pp. 491–542.

Lai, G 1999 Digging Up China: Nationalism, Politics, and the Yinxu Excavations, 1928–1937', paper presented at a panel on 'Sciences of the Human: Classicism, Modernism, and Nationalism in Chinese Social Sciences, 1899–1937. In The Fifty-first Annual Meeting of the Association for Asian Studies, Boston, 13 March 1999.

Lawton, T 1991 *A Time of Transition: Two Collectors of Chinese Art.* Lawrence: Spencer Museum of Art and the University of Kansas.

Li G 李光謨 1996 *Chutou kaoguxuejia de zuji – Li Ji zhixue shengya suoji* 鋤頭考古學家的足跡 – 李濟治學生涯瑣記. Beijing: Zhongguo renmin daxue chubanshe.

Li X 李曉東 1993 *Zhongguo wenwuxue gailun* 中國文物學概論. Shijiazhuang: Hebei renmin chubanshe.

Li X 李曉東 2013 *Minguo wenwu fagui shiping* 民國文物法規史評. Beijing: Wenwu chubanshe.

Lin J 林家平 Ning Q 寧強, and Luo H 羅華慶 1992 *Zhongguo Dunhuang xue shi* 中國敦煌學史 (A history of Dunhuang studies). Beijing: Beijing yuyan xueyuan chubanshe.

Liu Y 劉寅生and Yuan Y 袁英光 (eds.) 1984 *Wang Guowei quanji, shuxin* 王國維全集書信. Beijing: Zhonghua shuju.

Meng X 孟宪实 2004 Boxihe, Luo Zhenyu yu Dunhuang xue zhi chushi 伯希和、罗振玉与敦煌学之初始. *Duanhuang Tulufan yanjiu* 敦煌吐魯番研究, 7: 1–12.

Naquin, S 2000 *Peking: Temples and City Life, 1400–1900*. Berkeley: University of California Press.

Pai, I 2013 *Heritage Management in Korea and Japan: The Politics of Antiquity and Identity*. Seattle: University of Washington Press.

Qin S 2004 *Cultural Modernity: The Nantong Model, 1890–1930*. Stanford: Stanford University Press.

Ren D 任大山 2007 He Rizhang yu Henan bowuguan zaoqi jianshe 何日章與河南博物館早期建設. *Zhongyuan wenwu* 中原文物, 3: 106–108.

Rong X 榮新江 2001 *Dunhuangxue shiba jiang* 敦煌學十八講. Beijing: Beijing daxue chubanshe.

Schneider, L A 1971 *Ku Chieh-kang and China's New History: Nationalism and the Quest for Alternative Traditions*. Berkeley: University of California Press.

Shi, M 1998 From Imperial Gardens to Public Parks: the Transformation in Urban Space in the Early Twentieth Century Beijing. *Modern China,* 24 (3): 219–254.

Spence, J. D. 1990. *The Search for Modern China*. New York: W.W. Norton & Company.

Tian T 田濤 and Zheng Q 鄭秦 (eds.) 1999 *Da Qing lüli* 大清律例. Beijing: Falü chubanshe.

Tong L 2011 *A Passion for Facts: Social Surveys and the Construction of the Chinese Nation-State, 1900–1949*. Berkeley: University of California Press.

Wakeman, F Jr. 1975 *The Fall of Imperial China*. New York: Free Press.

Wang C-h 2010 The Qing Imperial Collection Circa 1905–25: National Humiliation Heritage Preservation and Exhibition Culture. In: Wu H (ed.) *Reinventing the Past: Archaism and Antiquarianism in Chinese Art and Visual Culture*. Chicago: The Center for the Art of East Asia, University of Chicago. pp. 320–341.

Wang J 王冀青 2007 1907 nian Sitanyin yu Wang Yuanlu ji Dunhuang guanyuan zhijian de jiaowang 1907年斯坦因與王圓祿及敦煌官員之間的交往. *Dunhuangxue jikan* 敦煌研究輯刊, 3: 60–76.

Wang J 王冀青 2011 Boxihe 1907 nian Beijing zhi xing xiangguan riqi bianzheng 伯希和1907年北京之行相關日期辯證.*Dunhuangxue jikan* 敦煌研究輯刊, 4: 139–144.

Wang R 汪榮祖 2006 *Zouxiang shijie de cuozhe: Guo Songtao yu Dao Xian Tong Guang shidai* 走向世界的挫折: 郭嵩濤與道咸同光時代. Beijing: Zhonghua shuju.

Wheaton, H 2000 *Huidun Wanguo gongfa*惠頓萬國公法, translated by Ding Weiliang 丁韪良. Beijing: Zhongguo zhengfa daxue chubanshe.

Yuan Y 袁英光and Liu Y 劉寅生 1996 *Wang Guowei nianpu changbian* 王國維年譜長編. Tianjin: Tianjin renmin chubanshe.

Ethnic heritage in Yunnan: contradictions and challenges

Fuquan Yang
Yunnan Academy of Social Sciences

Introduction

Yunnan is a province located in the far southwest of China, covering an area of 394,000 km^2. Its 4,000 km border adjoins Myanmar in the west, Laos in the south, and Vietnam in the southeast. Yunnan's population is just under 46 million (November 2010), of which 'ethnic minority communities (*shaoshu minzu*)' comprise roughly one third.

Tourism has become one of the four major industries in Yunnan (the other three being tobacco, mining, and agriculture); more

---

How to cite this book chapter:
Yang, F 2016 Ethnic heritage in Yunnan: contradictions and challenges. In: Matsuda, A and Mengoni, L E (eds.) *Reconsidering Cultural Heritage in East Asia*, Pp. 87–102. London: Ubiquity Press. DOI: http://dx.doi.org/10.5334/baz.e.

than 100,000 people were working in the tourism industry in the Lijiang Prefecture of Yunnan in 2010, when the total population was 1.25 million. Tourism based on 'ethnic heritage', in particular, has brought considerable economic benefits to many towns and villages in Yunnan, which used to be a largely poverty-stricken province (Yang 2006, 2007). The growth of tourism, however, has also commodified certain aspects of ethnic cultures, which has generated tensions and contradictions within local communities. This chapter examines these problems and outlines some pilot projects that seek to help resolve them and contribute towards sustainable development. While there are 26 ethnic groups in the province (including the Han), in this chapter I focus on the Naxi and Moso (also known as Na), with whom I have had a chance to work on various community-based cultural projects.[1]

Benefits of heritage-based tourism for ethnic minorities in Yunnan

The most popular heritage-based tourist destination in Yunnan is Lijiang, a prefecture-level city in the northwest part of the province. Lijiang's population is roughly 1.25 million (as of 2010), and the majority of its citizens are Naxi people. Lijiang is famous for its Old Town, which was designated a UNESCO heritage site in 1997 for having been the centre of silk embroidery in the southwest of China in ancient times. It was one of the most important places on the Ancient Caravan Road of Tea and Horses which extended from Yunnan to Sichuan, Tibet, and India. The architecture, culture, and history of Lijiang are quite unique in China.

It was only in the 1990s that the unique value of Lijiang was recognised by the provincial government, which decided to engage in an all-out effort to develop tourism in the city, leading to a staggering growth of revenue. Previously, Lijiang had been one of the poorest and most backward areas of the province. In the period from 1978 to 1988, while the annual GDP of Yunnan grew by an average of 9.1 percent, that of Lijiang grew by an average of only 1 percent, making it third from the bottom in the province. The growth in average annual revenue per person in Lijiang ranked fifth from bottom in the province in the same period. By 2010, however, the annual number of tourist visitors to Lijiang had reached 9.1 million, with 611,400 overseas tourists. Annual tourism revenue reached 11.2 billion yuan, or roughly 1.7 billion US dollars, and foreign exchange earnings from tourism in 2010 had reached 1.4 billion yuan (202 million US dollars). In 2010 the city's cultural industries earned 1.5 billion yuan (218 million US dollars), over three times more than they had in 2005, accounting for a rise in GDP from 8.6 percent to 11.8 percent in this period. In 2012, the GDP of Lijiang was 15.0 billion yuan (2.4 billion US dollars), and total tourism revenue reached 11.2 billion yuan (1.8 billion US dollars) (Statistical Bulletin of the National Economic and Social Development in Lijiang n.d.; Yang 2012b).

Lijiang currently has eight travel agencies and 100 tourist information centres (*lüyouxingxiangdian*, literally 'tourism image stores') nationwide, located in major cities. The 27 travel agencies that previously existed have been integrated into six business groups and today each group manages a particular geographic area with the aim of avoiding excessive competition and friction and creating a safe and orderly market environment.

The following two examples illustrate the success of ethnic tourism in Lijiang. The first is the example of the Dayan Naxi Ancient Music Association located in the Lijiang Old Town. This Association was formed in 1989, with an orchestra comprising teachers, workers, farmers, artisans, and craftsmen, and has since become famous for its 'three old things': old music, old musicians, and old musical instruments. By 2007 the orchestra's annual revenue exceeded five million yuan, roughly 650,000 US dollars. Despite the relatively high price of the tickets, 160 yuan (roughly 21 US dollars), the orchestra has large audiences at its daily performances, which have become a regular element of Lijiang's visitor attractions. The orchestra has also performed in many larger cities in China, including Beijing, Shanghai, Tianjin, and Guangzhou, and in over 20 countries overseas. It also performed in the celebrations held in Beijing in 2005 to mark the 60th anniversary of the founding of the United Nations.

The second example is various 'cultural villages' existing in Lijiang which attract tourists with the chance to experience the rural life of the Naxi and Moso people, including village ceremonies, traditional houses and barns, and the opportunity to interact with young and old residents. The most popular of these villages is arguably Luoshui village, located in Lijiang's Nangling County. A collection of highly picturesque wooden Moso homes and guesthouses on the shore of Lake Lugu, to the northwest of Lijiang, this village was at one time extremely poor due to the scant amount of land available for farming. The ethnic tourism that took off in the 1990s brought considerable economic benefits, making it now one of the ten wealthiest villages in Lijiang. A committee made up of residents manages all tourism-related activities in the village, including taking guests to scenic spots by boat and horse. Aiming to avoid unregulated competition and to maintain equity and fairness, the committee has drawn up rules that prohibit or restrict tourism activities that run counter to traditional ways of life. It has even attempted to introduce rules designed to preserve and shore up the matrilineality of its society (Yang 2005).

Re-energising and protecting ethnic minority culture

In earlier periods of Chinese history, the majority Chinese often regarded ethnic minority cultures as primitive, backward, and barbaric. This was a view particularly prevalent amongst the ruling classes and urban dwellers, as attested by many accounts in official records, especially those written in the Qing dynasty (1644–1912).

Ethnic heritage-based tourism initiated in Yunnan in the 1990s has helped build wider appreciation of ethnic minority cultures in China, and at the same time has helped these communities nurture pride in their own heritage. The integration of ethnic cultures and tourism has clearly increased the awareness of the value of ethnic heritage in Yunnan amongst people in government and business, as well as artist groups. Whether ethnic cultures are perceived as a draw for tourism or valuable in their own right, this movement has clearly contributed to a flourishing of indigenous cultures.

There is now a particular interest in the ancient Dongba culture associated with the Naxi people, the most famous examples of which include religious manuscripts, music, and painting. Dongba culture has today become one of the major tourist attractions in rural and urban areas of Yunnan (and also Sichuan province to the north). Today, one can find Dongba calligraphy or Dongba-style paintings hanging in local houses, or lines or words from Dongba poetry inscribed on the pillars of front gates of various buildings.

In Yunnan some grand-scale ethnic dance performances have emerged from the confluence of tourism and ethnic cultures. One of such performances is called 'Dynamic Yunnan' (*Yunnan*

Yingxiang) and features the dancer and choreographer Yang Liping, a member of the Bai ethnic community. Another performance, entitled 'Impression Lijiang' (*Yinxiang Lijiang*) and first played in 2006, is an open-air folk musical directed by the internationally renowned film director Zhang Yimou and staged at the foot of Yulong Xueshan, a mountain massif near Lijiang. Both performances draw strongly on ethnic traditions, and the majority of the performers are from ethnic minority communities.

Both the national and provincial governments have enacted regulations to protect and promote ethnic heritage. In 2000, the national Regulations on the Protection of Traditional Folk Culture in Yunnan was established, which was the first of a kind in China. In 2006 the Standing Committee of the National People's Congress enacted provincial level regulations, which are known collectively as the Regulations on the Protection of Dongba Cultures and designed to protect Naxi ethnic heritage. Meanwhile, the Yunnan government initiated a census on folk cultures in Yunnan and their intangible heritage between 2000 and 2002 with funding from the Ford Foundation. These legal and administrative frameworks have facilitated the conservation of ethnic heritage in Yunnan (Yang 2010).

The increased awareness of the value of cultural heritage in Yunnan has also led the national government to promote it internationally. As stated, Lijiang Old Town was inscribed on UNESCO's World Heritage List in 1997. In addition, the Ancient Naxi Dongba Pictographic Manuscripts were inscribed on UNESCO's World Memory List in 2003, and the Cultural Landscape of Honghe Hani Rice Terraces in Southern Yunnan – an area of 16,603 ha of rice terraces developed on mountain slopes and attributed to the Hani people in Yuanyang County – was registered on the World Heritage List in 2013.

Problems in the conservation of ethnic heritage

While tourism has brought significant economic prosperity to Yunnan since the mid-1990s, the penetration of a commodity-based economy has generated tensions and contradictions. One of the consequences of commercialisation in Lijiang is that many local residents, particularly those in the Old Town, are increasingly renting out their homes and staring to live elsewhere, drawn by the profit that can be earned by leasing properties and also by the wish to avoid the crowds and noise (Yang 2004). Most of the new residents arrive to run businesses or simply for leisure. Often they are not interested in traditional Naxi culture, particularly in learning the Naxi language.

This change marks a real difference from how Lijiang has been historically. The city has seen waves of migration from other regions of China for centuries; a 1950 survey of the 156 surnames of residents in Lijiang Old Town revealed how immigrants from many different parts of China came to live in the town, especially during the Ming (1368–1644) and Qing Dynasties (1644–1912). In the past, however, these incoming groups tended to blend in with the Naxi people and their cultures (Yang 2012b).

The lack of integration of currently incoming groups into the local culture creates an alarming situation, as Naxi tradition seems in fact to be in decline. By 2003, the last three great Dongba master priests, who were living repositories of knowledge on Dongba culture – particularly the highly complex Dongba writing system which is said to take at least ten years to master – had died, leaving no comparable successors. In the 1980s, the Yunnan government started funding the translation and publication of 1,000 Naxi manuscripts, and nearly 20 Dongba priests and 10 scholars worked on this endeavour for over 20 years. Little attention was, however, directed to the training of younger priests, and today there are very few qualified Dongba priests who are able to translate various Dongba manuscripts housed in museums and university libraries around the world as skilfully as their former master priests. How to train Dongba master priests is a crucial question for the Naxi people, as it involves the passing of Dongba cultural, intellectual, and religious heritage on to future generations.

Surely it would be impossible to force Naxi residents to stay in Lijiang Old Town. It would be equally impossible to force incoming residents to learn about the local culture and to conserve the Naxi language. The changing composition of the current population in Lijiang – and indeed throughout Yunnan province – is gradually affecting traditional customs and practices; it clearly endangers the authenticity and vitality of Naxi culture as a whole.

Traditional Moso culture is similarly under threat. One of the most interesting features of the Moso people is the strongly matrilineal nature of their society and the related 'visiting relations' system (*zou hun* in Chinese; *ti se se* in the Moso language), in which sexual partners do not live in the same household. The majority of the Moso people wish to conserve their matrilineal tradition, and have even sought to have it registered on UNESCO's List of Intangible Cultural Heritage. However, conservation is likely to prove difficult with the seemingly unstoppable march of modernisation; marriage is gaining in popularity, and today the right to marry the person one chooses is naturally seen as a human right. Young Moso people are increasingly going farther afield to find work in urban areas, which is inevitably affecting traditional customs. Similarly, people from other communities and areas move into Moso villages to run commercial enterprises, with an inevitable effect on indigenous kinship. Villages like Luoshui and Lige, the main attraction of which lies in the fact that they are Moso villages, are following the example of Lijiang Old Town. More and more local people now rent their family-run inns to people from outside the villages, instead of running them themselves.

Luoshui village has attempted to preserve the traditional organisation of its large matrilineal families through a series of measures, including the so-called 'one fire place, one person' policy. Aiming to prevent the weakening of local customs, the policy limits the number of persons per family who are allowed to take part in village-run tourism activities. Despite such efforts, there are growing numbers of families where partners live under the same roof and run along 'nuclear' lines.

Another recent phenomenon is the increase of young people of ethnic minority background from rural areas, particularly women, who go to urban areas in search of work. This has given rise to serious problems for the conservation and continuation of village traditions. As the composition of rural society changes, with more elderly people and fewer women left behind, it is becoming difficult to preserve person-to-person transmission of intangible cultural heritage. This is symptomatic of the broader challenge of conserving intangible cultural heritage in China today, where modernization and urbanization are proceeding apace.

Erosion of traditional value systems and lifestyles, loss of intangible cultural heritage, and commodification of religion and culture are by-products of economic development brought by tourism. Tangible cultural heritage, particularly architecture, has also been affected. In Lijiang Old Town, for example, some new residents who are renting Naxi houses for commercial purposes have replaced their architectural features with those of the traditional Han style, assuming that it is acceptable because both architectural features are 'traditional'. In other cases, local people have replaced traditional buildings with modern ones, influenced by urban styles seen on television. The case in point is the five traditional villages in the Xishuangbanna autonomous region in southern Yunnan, which had a tourist attraction rating of 4A according to the China National Tourism Standard Association's standards (the highest being 5A). Once the local villagers experienced the economic benefits brought by tourism development, they started building Western-style villas alongside their traditional bamboo dwellings, which immediately triggered tourist complaints and criticisms (Yang 2013).

This last example highlights the problems inherent in the conservation of traditional buildings in tourist villages: one might consider that Western-style buildings incongruous with village traditions should ideally be avoided, but it would also be unfair to ask villagers to keep living in traditional bamboo buildings without proper sanitary facilities just for the sake of attracting tourists. Thought must be given to suitable ways to refurbish the traditional village architecture, so that living conditions can be improved inside buildings without affecting their outside appearance. Researchers, architects, and planners also have to think in more far-reaching ways about encouraging an appreciation and understanding of the cultural and spiritual value of traditional architecture among residents (Yang 2010).

All this points to an urgent need for the development of sustainable forms of ethnic tourism, which aims for the conservation of the vitality of ethnic cultures. For this to happen, the active inclusion of ethnic minorities is vital.

Pilot projects for cultural heritage conservation in Lijiang

I have led and participated in a number of pilot projects designed to explore best practice for the conservation of ethnic heritage in

Yunnan, especially the heritage of the Naxi Dongba culture. These projects were concerned with: the training of future Dongba priests; the training of young practitioners of traditional music; the promotion of young people's interest in indigenous knowledge and traditional folk customs; and the training of women in traditional handicrafts, particularly embroidery.

The first of these projects, aimed at training Dongba priests, ran from 2000 to 2003 in Lijiang, with the financial support of the Beijing Office of the Ford Foundation. The project group selected eight students from several villages that have particularly rich Dongba traditions; some of the students were sons and grandsons of Dongba priests. Experienced Dongba masters then offered training to the students in accordance with traditional training methods, with the assistance of researchers at the Dongba Culture Research Institute. The Dongba masters and the students lived together during the training. The students were required to learn manuscripts by heart and to study Dongba rituals, writings, singing, and dancing, and how to construct the materials used in rituals such as facial masks, painted wooden tablets, and ritual offerings. They also had to undertake regular and rigorous examinations. At certain intervals they then went back to their villages for several months to practice what they had learnt and to acquire more folk knowledge from their village elders. This project proved quite successful, and many of the students have since become respected priests in Lijiang.

The second project, which ran from 2001 to 2004, aimed at encouraging young musicians to learn how to perform one of the two surviving forms of traditional music, Baisha Xiyue, which is a kind of classical orchestral music dating from the Yuan Dynasty (1271–1368), involving flutes, shawms, lutes, and zithers. Baisha Xiyue is said to represent a merging of Mongol palace music and

Naxi music. The story goes that in 1253 Kublai Han presented the Naxi ruler Mailiang with an orchestra when Mailiang welcomed him at Fengke. When the pilot project was initiated, there were very few surviving musicians who could play this music. The project team worked with the master musician He Maogen, an officially recognised descendent of a long line of Baisha Xiyue musicians, who had also trained his son He Linyi and his nephew over many years so that both could become outstanding musicians.

The third project, which was supported by the Beijing Office of the Ford Foundation, had as its objective the teaching of local knowledge relating to Naxi cultural heritage to primary school children in rural areas. The idea underlying the project was to promote the transfer of basic knowledge of tangible and intangible cultural heritage from childhood. As its first site the project team selected the Baisha Primary School in Baisha Town, Yulong County. The training was based on a participatory methodology; teachers, students and their parents, and project researchers all took part. The stakeholders in the project, including researchers, government officials, villagers, school teachers, and students and their parents, discussed together what kind of local knowledge one should learn and what methods should be used for that purpose. The project participants sought to introduce experimental education and link it to the government plan for the promotion and education of local knowledge. We carried out fieldwork together with teachers and students to investigate community resources, including landscape, forests, rivers, agriculture, history, and folklore, conducted interviews with local elders, craftsmen, herb healers, and other community members, and invited folk singers and elders to give lectures to the students. Thereafter, the project group compiled and edited a textbook to be used by students and teachers in the community. We also selected and used students' paintings in the Dongba pictographic style in another textbook edited by the Ministry of Education, which was designed to teach local knowledge. Similar projects were also carried out in primary schools, the intake of which comprised the children of Tibetan and Dai ethic minority groups. Here again, the participants included teachers and students, local educational officers, and scholars of the Yunnan Academy of Social Sciences.

The fourth project was designed to counteract the decline in the knowledge of handicrafts in rural areas, particularly embroidery. My team carried out a four-year project in Baihua, a Naxi village in Huangshan Township, Lijiang, in order to train ethnic minority women in traditional handicrafts, with the support of Misereor, a Catholic charitable foundation funded by the German Federal Ministry for Economic Cooperation and Development. Trained by knowledgeable elders, more than 15 women of various communities, including the Naxi, Moso, Lisu, Tibetan, and Bai, learned how to produce attractive handicrafts involving weaving, embroidery, and dyeing with traditional natural materials. They earned enough money to improve their living conditions in only a few years, and are now teaching their skills to other young women.

This last project also provided an insight into how to combine the production of traditional handicrafts with the demands of the modern market. The key seems to lie in maintaining distinctive local characteristics. Innovation is possible in terms of deciding what kind of items to be produced – for example, silk scarves which tend to have an appeal to young people – but tradition can be maintained in the use of the patterns and designs distinct to the locality (Yang 2012a).

Conclusion

The current state of cultural heritage varies significantly from one ethnic community to another in Yunnan province. Within the wider climate of social change, some communities have developed heritage-based tourism rather successfully. The orchestra of the Dayan Naxi Ancient Music Association, for example, has greatly benefited from tourism development. At the same time, however, the changing social and economic conditions are threatening the heritage of other ethnic communities. For instance, some folk music in rural areas is in decline, especially music that involves improvisation. Also, despite our best efforts, many aspects of knowledge of Dongba culture, in particular writing and religious rituals, are gradually disappearing. The conservation of such forms of living cultural heritage poses a big challenge as it requires large amounts of time, energy, and commitment.

Notwithstanding the considerable attention now being directed to the conservation of ethnic cultural heritage in Yunnan, both on provincial and national levels, many problems still remain. Balancing between gaining economic benefits and maintaining the core value of cultural heritage is a particularly challenging task. Cultural heritage is an important attraction for tourism that can bring much needed alleviation to poverty-stricken areas, but it is also a sensitive asset that can be damaged by the same tourism. Achieving the sustainable conservation of cultural heritage is a pressing and important issue in Yunnan. In order to make informed judgement about how to achieve such sustainable conservation, more action research based on pilot projects needs to be carried out.

Note

[1] Although the Chinese government categorises the Naxi and Moso peoples as being in the same ethnic minority, researchers generally agree that they are culturally distinct. While broadly sharing the same historic origin, the Naxi and Moso cultures have developed differently over time. The chief distinguishing characteristics of the Moso people include the strongly matriarchal and matrilineal aspects of their society.

References

Statistical Bulletin of the National Economic and Social Development in Lijiang (n.d.) http://www.lijiang.cn/ (accessed on 1 September 2015).

Yang F 2004 Some problems of Tourism Development in Yunnan. *Social Sciences in Yunnan,* 3.

Yang F 2005 *A Plan for Lijiang: Tourism and Culture.* Beijing: Ethnic Nationalities Press (Minzu Press).

Yang F 2006 *The Reports of Yunnan Tourism Development (Annual Blue Books), 2005–2006.* Kunming: Yunnan University Press.

Yang F 2007 *The Reports of Yunnan Tourism Development (Annual Blue Books), 2006–2007.* Kunming: Yunnan University Press.

Yang F 2010 *Conservation and Development of Famous Towns and Villages of Yunnan.* Beijing: Zhongguo Shuji Chubanshe (China Book Publishers).

Yang F 2012a. The practice of mentorship of ethnic folk cultural heritage and challenges in Lijiang. In *The Collection of Papers on the latest development and Practice of Applied Anthropology in China.* July. Beijing: Ethnic Nationalities Press (Minzu Press).

Yang F 2012b *A Brief History of Contemporary Naxi.* Kumming: Yunnan People's Publishing House.

Yang F 2013 Seeking the Balance between Ethnic Cultural Resources and Development of Cultural Industry. Making Yunnan as an Example. *Journal of Minzu University of China* (Philosophy and Social Sciences Edition), 2.

Cultural heritage in Korea – from a Japanese perspective

Toshio Asakura
National Museum of Ethnology

Introduction

The Korean television drama *Dae Jang-geum* has been popular not only in Korea but also throughout East Asia, including in Japan, Taiwan and China. It is based on the true story of Jang-geum, the reputedly first woman to hold the position of royal physician in the 16th-century during the Joseon Dynasty (1392–1897). What is interesting about the drama from a perspective of cultural heritage is that it serves to highlight traditional Korean culture, especially Korean court cuisine and medicine.

How to cite this book chapter:
Asakura, T 2016 Cultural heritage in Korea – from a Japanese perspective. In: Matsuda, A and Mengoni, L E (eds.) *Reconsidering Cultural Heritage in East Asia*, Pp. 103–119. London: Ubiquity Press. DOI: http://dx.doi.org/10.5334/baz.f.

I was in charge of supervising the Japanese-language version of this show, and one of the most challenging, yet interesting, aspects of my task was to work out how to translate Korean culture to a Japanese audience.[1] By referring to this drama, which was part of the so-called 'Korean wave' (*hanryû*), I will investigate the circumstances surrounding three aspects of cultural heritage in Korea: culinary culture; Living National Treasures (i.e. holders of Important Intangible Cultural Properties); and cultural landscapes. Japan and Korea are said to share broadly similar cultural heritage, including amongst other things the influence of Chinese culture, as exemplified by the spoken language and script, and the influence of Confucianism. However, through comparison with Japan I will attempt to reveal some of the more distinct characteristics of cultural heritage in Korea, and also make a few suggestions pertinent to the discussion of cultural heritage in the East Asian context.

Culinary culture

Jang-geum, the protagonist in *Dae Jang-geum,* was based on a historical figure whose name appears in the *Joseon Wangjo Sillok*, the annual records of the Joseon Dynasty kept from 1413 until 1865. In the first half of the drama series, she appears as a lady of the court, responsible for preparing royal court cuisine. This is, however, a fictitious representation of her because the historical Jang-geum was a royal physician and did not perform such tasks. The reason behind this historically inaccurate rendering in the drama can be attributed to the concept in Korean culture known as *yaksikdongwon*, which claims that health is maintained by a combination of food and medical treatment.

While the popularity of the drama *Dae Jang-geum* can be explained by several factors, one of the most important factors is undoubtedly the growing interest in food in Korean society.[2] The restaurant industry is currently developing fast in Korea, which is in part thanks to the contribution of many different foreign cuisines but is also due to the recent re-appreciation of the traditional Korean foods as being beneficial to health, the best example of which is 'court cuisine'.[3] Court cuisine offers something different from full-course traditional meals called *hanjeongsik*, which have long been available at many Korean restaurants. Court cuisine is, in fact, a brand developed by Hwang Hye-seong (1920–2006), who is designated as a holder of Important Intangible Cultural Properties, informally known as a Living National Treasure, in recognition of her skill in Korean royal court cuisine (Moon 2009). When Hwang Hye-seong began teaching Korean cuisine at Sookmyung Women's University in 1942, she was encouraged by the director of the University, Oda Shôgo, to study court cuisine, which at the time was on the verge of disappearing (Hwang & Ishige 1988). She subsequently learned court cuisine from the last *sanggun* (court lady) in charge of cooking for the royal family, compiled its recipes, expounded it in a scholarly manner, developed it in a way suitable to contemporary life, and made it known to the world (An 2007). She founded the restaurant Jihwaja, located across from Unhyeon Palace in Seoul, which serves to bring court cuisine of the Joseon Dynasty to everyday people. In keeping with this strongly heritage-based approach to cuisine, the homepage of Jihwaja's website is entitled *The Culinary Culture of the House of Hwang Hye-seong*, and includes sections entitled 'The "Korean Royal Court Cuisine" of the 38th National Important Intangible Cultural Property', and 'People at the House of Hwang Hye-seong'.

This reconsideration of traditional cuisine has been linked with a national movement promoting the globalization of Korean food,[4] one of the most prominent examples of which is the 'Japan–Korea Kimchi War'. *Kimchi* is perhaps the most well-recognized Korean food around the globe, but in the mid-1990s it emerged that Korean *kimchi* was losing out to Japanese produced *kimchi* (or *kimuchi*, which is the Japanese pronunciation) in world markets. Following this news, in 1996 at a meeting of the International Food Standards Agency (CODEX), the Korean Ministry for Food, Agriculture, Forestry and Fisheries claimed that *kimchi* is a food that is naturally fermented, and therefore flavour-enhanced Japanese *kimchi* prepared with additives is not real *kimchi*. This controversy was widely publicized by the Japanese media in the summer of 1999 as the 'Japan–Korea Kimchi War'. This development appears to have been the first step in Korea's efforts to reaffirm *kimchi*'s status in the World as a traditional and culturally Korean food (Asakura 2009).

As a way of improving Korea's national brand value through culture, President Lee Myung-bak decided to promote Korean food both domestically and abroad, and established the Korean Food Globalization Promotion Committee in 2009 and enacted a law to promote the restaurant industry in 2011. President Lee's wife, Kim Yoon-ok, became the honorary president of the Korean Food Globalization Promotion Committee and aimed to establish Korean food as one of the top five cuisines in the World, with particular emphasis on promoting *bibimbap*, a traditional rice dish with cooked vegetables.[5] President Lee also sought personally to further the export of *makkeolli*, a traditional Korean liquor. In this way, Korea engaged in a worldwide strategy to spread Korean food as culture.

Let us now consider the contrasting circumstances in Japan with regards to the globalization of food. Japanese food has already been well known in various places in the World for some time, and increasing numbers of restaurants have been opening outside of Japan claiming to offer 'Japanese food', which however generally fails to resemble authentic Japanese cuisine.[6] In response to this situation, in 2006 the Japanese Ministry of Agriculture, Forestry and Fisheries attempted to formulate a system of evaluating the authenticity of menus that claim to offer Japanese food.[7] This move, however, received opposition both inside and outside of Japan. The Ministry subsequently decided to give up on the idea of establishing a governmental system for authenticating Japanese food and leave the matter to be dealt with by the private sector. Admitting the difficulty of providing a definition of 'Japanese food', the Ministry acknowledged that 'ingredients and methods of preparation should be determined by the practice in each country, and private evaluating organizations should be organized by food researchers in the actual locations' (Shimbun 2007).

In Japan, dietary culture has tended to be transmitted under private leadership. A notable example of this is the annual Kyoto Food Exhibition, which began in 1876 by owners of famous restaurants and still continues today. Another example can be found in the way in which new forms of dietary culture, such as gifting chocolate for Valentine's Day and eating rolled sushi during the Setsubun Festival held on February 3rd, have been generated and promoted by private business initiatives. This type of private leadership in Japanese food culture presents a strong contrast to Korea's recent tendency towards top-down governmental leadership.

The question that I would like to raise at this point is: to what extent can and should food be considered as part of cultural heritage? Although food may be part of material culture, it is perishable, and once consumed by people, it turns into human waste. In other words, unlike other types of material culture, food is difficult to maintain because it cannot be preserved in its original form and changes according to location and period. Food can, nevertheless, be described and preserved in written documents, and techniques of preparation can be handed down. Chinese and Japanese dietary culture has already spread worldwide, and Korea is fighting for a place in this development. In view of this, it would be reasonable to consider whether more attention should be given to food as cultural heritage in the East Asian context.

Living National Treasures (holders of Important Intangible Cultural Properties)

During the production of the drama *Dae Jang-geum,* the person responsible for providing dietary research was Han Bok-ryeo (1947–present), the eldest daughter of Hwang Hye-seong, discussed previously. In 2007, a year after Hwang Hye-seong passed away, Han Bok-ryeo became the third Living National Treasure in the field of royal court cuisine. The first person to be given this title in 1971 was Hwang Hye-seong's teacher, Han Hee-sun (1889–1972), who was also the model for Jang-geum's teacher in the television drama. At the age of twelve, Han Hee-sun started working in a position in the court's outer kitchen, but after ten years rose to the position of *sanggun* (court lady) of the inner kitchen and became responsible for preparing the royal meals for Emperor Gojong, Crown Prince Sunjong, and Lady Yoon. She lived at court until 1950, when Lady Yoon fled to Busan at the outbreak of the Korean War. Thereafter, Han Hee-sun taught court cuisine twice a week at Sookmyung Women's University (Ye 1976).

In 1962, the Korean Cultural Properties Protection Act was enacted to provide legal protection to four categories of cultural properties: tangible cultural properties; intangible cultural properties; monuments; and folk resources.[8] According to the law, both the national and local governments can designate cultural properties to be protected, and the intangible cultural properties that are given a national designation are called 'Important Intangible Cultural Properties'.

As of December 2009, there were 114 nationally designated Important Intangible Cultural Properties, and its breakdown was as follows: in the field of performance arts, there were 17 for music, 7 for dance, 14 for theatre, 24 for ceremonies and types of popular entertainment, and 1 for martial arts; in the field of technical arts, there were 49 for crafts, and 2 for cuisine. The number of individuals designated as holders of these Important Intangible Cultural Properties was 184. On the local governmental level, on the other hand, there were 388 designated intangible cultural properties, and 470 individuals were designated as their holders (Chŏng 2009).

Korea has been active in not only protecting but also promoting its intangible cultural properties. For instance, the National Research Institute of Cultural Heritage, which is affiliated with the Cultural Heritage Administration of Korea (Chŏng 2009), has produced a series of books and videos to introduce the Important Intangible Cultural Properties in Korean and English. Additionally, the Bucheon World Intangible Cultural Heritage Expo, hosted by Bucheon City and supported by the Ministry of Culture, Sports and Tourism, was held in 2008 to 2010 to present intangible cultural properties from Korea and around the World.

In Korea, as in Japan, individuals designated as holders of Important Intangible Cultural Properties are popularly called 'Living National Treasures' or 'Living Cultural Properties', and they have a clearly recognised role in popular consciousness. Japan's Living National Treasures are selected for skills in the performance arts of court dance (*gagaku*), *noh* theatre, puppet theatre (*bunraku*), *kabuki*, traditional Ryûkyû narrative dance (*kumi-odori*), music, Japanese dance (*buyô*), *engei* and theatre; as well as for skills in the technical arts of ceramics, dyeing and weaving, Japanese stencil-making (*Ise-katagami*), lacquer, metalwork, sword making, doll making, woodwork, and paper making. Korea has more categories of Important Intangible Cultural Properties than Japan, extending even to cuisine and martial arts, and the number of their holders – namely Living National Treasures – is also greater (184 as of December 2009 as stated earlier). Recently, however, the increased numbers of Living National Treasures has generated a challenge to the transmission of the recognised skills for future generations in Korea (Koreana 1997: 13). This issue is in part related to the fact that, unlike Japan where generational succession to a family trade is fairly common and has a long history, in Korea the generational succession of traditional practitioners does not tend to be very strong. Consequently, the government needs to support traditional practitioners more actively in Korea than in Japan.

Since the end of the Korean War in 1953, there have been ongoing efforts in Korea to re-evaluate traditional practices and beliefs that were ignored and denigrated under the shadow of modernization. Many traditional folk practices and rural performances have consequently been uncovered, preserved, and designated as intangible cultural properties; even shamans and their rituals which were dismissed as superstitious until recently have now been protected with national and local designations. In this sense, the protection of intangible cultural properties in Korea has been more wide-ranging than in Japan.

At this point it is worth remembering that very few countries around the World have a system of designating and protecting intangible cultural properties. In view of this, it seems important to examine why the protection and promotion of intangible cultural properties has become a national policy in Japan and Korea in relation to the global discourse of cultural heritage.

Cultural landscapes

Han Bok-ryeo is currently the director of the Institute of Korean Royal Cuisine that is located in the area of Bukchon in Seoul, and she also runs a restaurant named Gungyeon which she opened in 2003 in Bukchon. Bukchon literally means 'Northern Village', and it was so named because of its location to the north of Jongno, which was historically the centre of Hanyang (the name for Seoul during the Joseon Period) and the River Cheonggyecheon. Bukchon is often dubbed the 'Korean Village' because a group of *hanok*, traditional Korean dwellings, still survive there. Historically, Bukchon stands between the Gyeongbokgung Palace and the Changdeokgung Palace, and used to be a place of residence for members of the royal family and powerful noble families known as *yangban*.

During the 1970s, the Korean government undertook many development works in the Gangnam District, a different area in Seoul, and this resulted in a few of the country's oldest schools in Bukchon being transferred to Gangnam. The area in Bukchon that used to be occupied by these schools now came to be occupied by newly built big modern buildings, the most famous of which are the headquarters of the Hyundai group and the Constitutional Court of Korea. This triggered a movement for preserving the traditional landscape characterised by the *hanok* and promoting traditional cultural activities in Bukchon. As a result, the area has been culturally revitalised and become a place of residence for artists and business and political leaders, with its traditional craft workshops and museums marking it out as a tourist destination.

In contrast to Bukchon, the area of Pimatgol in Seoul has lost its traditional landscape almost entirely. Pimatgol has its origins in the Joseon dynasty, when it developed along a street that ran in parallel with the major avenue Jongno; the street of Pimatgol was built for common people trying to avoid the traffic of government and court officials riding on horseback on Jongno. The street was for a long time famous for its line of restaurants where people could satisfy their appetites and quench their thirst in their everyday life. However, in 2003, permission was granted to redevelop the area, and construction of skyscrapers began. Voices were then raised for the heritage protection of Pimatgol, and in 2004 guidelines were published in support of the historical preservation of the area. The guidelines, however, had little effect, and all the traces of Pimatgol except the street itself have disappeared.[9]

The loss of a characteristic cultural landscape has been observed not only in Pimatgol but also many other places across Korea. In 1993, the Korean art historian Hong-jun Yu (2000: 3) reflected on Korean heritage as a whole and made the following observation:

> 'The entire Korean peninsula is a museum…[it] is so small…The passage of history is carved into this small land, so wherever one travels here, one encounters examples of tangible and intangible cultural heritage. From glorious royal lands to villages hidden in deep mountains, these examples of cultural heritage have lost none of their vigour but are firmly alive'.

Despite this observation, like most parts of the World Korea has experienced the desire and the need for economic development and modernisation, often acting against preservation of traditional landscapes. In particular, under its military government

(1961–1987) Korea saw a high degree of economic development, which came to be dubbed 'the Miracle of the Han River', and continued to accelerate even after the change to a democratic government.

The rapid and often abrupt changes in many cultural landscapes, both rural and urban, that have taken place in Korea over the last several decades were noted by the Japanese historian and cultural essayist Yomota Inuhiko, who visited Korea for the first time from 1979 to 1980, and then in 2000. On his second visit he wrote: 'It has completely changed. The entire Seoul port that I used to know has somehow become an object for nostalgia' (Yomota 2001: 2, 52). During this short period of time, the appearance of Seoul had been completely transformed.[10] With this in mind, I would like to raise the issue of landscape conservation and restoration.

In Japan, along with the conservation of urban landscape (as practiced at Kanazawa and Uji), there has recently been much re-appreciation of the importance of landscapes closely associated with the daily lives and customs of local people, including those living near terraced rice fields and within mountain villages (*satoyama*). In 2005, the Japanese Law for the Protection of Cultural Properties was revised to adopt a new category 'cultural landscapes' with the aim of giving legal protection to the nationally designated 'Important Cultural Landscapes' (see Mouri's chapter in this book). Recently, Korea has also endeavoured to recognize the importance of urban landscapes through such projects as the restoration of the River Cheonggyecheon and the Gyeongbokgung Palace in Seoul. However, the conservation of rural landscapes that have evolved in association with the livelihood and customs of the local population are still in the course of development.

As globalization continues, the risk of losing historically developed cultural landscapes to monotonous and often sterile new sights increases. Asian cities have various faces – some are disordered, and some are aesthetically mediocre. Should such unimpressive faces be allowed to disappear for the sake of improving landscapes? If those faces are also to be considered examples of cultural heritage, then in what form should they be preserved?

Conclusion

In this chapter, I have compared Korea and Japan in connection with three topics: culinary culture, Living National Treasures, and cultural landscapes. To Japanese eyes, in contrast to Japan, cultural heritage in Korea has developed 'from the top', dynamically and rapidly. What might account for this difference? Both Korea and Japan have since ancient times been influenced by Chinese civilization, including the culture of Chinese characters and Confucianism. Geo-politically speaking, however, they are different in that Korea is a peninsula whereas Japan is an archipelago. Moreover, the Korean peninsula has a long history of dynastic rule; for example, during the Joseon dynasty, Confucianism was treated as orthodoxy and the literati ruling class governed the country for five hundred years – from the 14th-century onward. By contrast, in Japan from the 16th-century, although Confucianism served as the ideology of rulership, warriors held power and a social system based on Confucian principles did not emerge. Confucian principles underpinned the social system on the Korean peninsula, and they continue to inform society and daily life in Korea today, meaning that conditions there are somewhat different from those in Japan.

During the early modern period (ca. early 1500s to late 1800s), the Korean peninsula was ruled by a centralized government in the form of the long-established Joseon dynasty. This form of centralized government persisted well into modern times when Korea fell under military rule during the colonial period (1910–1945). By contrast, prior to the establishment of an 'enlightened state' during the modern period, Japan operated under the *bakufu* (military government) system of regionally divided power during the Edo period (1600–1868). Although a 'warrior-farmer-tradesman-merchant' class system was in place at this time in Japan, praise was awarded to anyone who succeeded in his particular field, regardless of class. On the other hand, society on the Korean peninsula was built around an agricultural economy in which anyone who made a living by special skills outside agriculture tended to be despised. For this reason, people with culinary skills have traditionally been respected in Japan and this has made way for eating and drinking establishments to develop into family businesses; whereas in Korea this was not traditionally the case so such establishments tend only to span one generation.

Japan and Korea also display differences in regard to interest in material culture:

> 'Based on the Confucian nature-as-principle teaching which served as the fundamental ideology of the literati ruling class during the Joseon dynasty, a human-centred world-view prevailed in which personal introspection was valued, and external material culture, technology, trade and consumption tended to be neglected. There was little discussion regarding the relationship between human beings and things that are not human beings' (Itô 2003: 13).

The difference appears in the single word 'thing'. The Japanese word for 'thing' (*mono*) can be used in many different ways, and no equivalent can be found for it in Korean.[11]

Following from these historical and cultural conditions, one economic policy has been promoted in Korea since the colonial period and the war, 'to pursue and overtake Japan'. On the other hand, a cultural policy has also been worked out to uncover and protect traditional culture.[12] National strategy has been to create a revitalised traditional culture, to promote culture, and so to generate new forms of cultural heritage. In this respect it seems to me that the creation of new forms of cultural heritage is more likely to occur in Korea than in Japan.

Notes

1 I am an ethnologist, and became involved in supervising a historical drama because it was thought that I could provide something different from the information available through historical research; in particular explaining history from a contemporary perspective.

2 One indication of the interest in food is the many gourmet cooking programs on Korean television. Also, the cartoon *Sikgaek* (The Gourmet) is popular in Korea and has been turned into a movie (like Japan's *Oishinbo*).

3 Neither Japan, which has an emperor, nor England, which has a queen, has a royal 'court cuisine'. Royal court cuisine can exist in Korea perhaps, ironically, because the country no longer has a royal court.

4 Throughout 2009, the Korean newspaper *Joong Ang Daily* published articles about the plan for the 'globalisation of Korean food'.

5 The globalisation of *bibimbap* is discussed in Kuroda Katsuhiro's critical essay 'What is the Burden of *Bibimbap*?' published in *Sankei Shimbun* (26 December 2009). Koreans objected to the essay, and Kuroda responded with another essay in *Sankei Shimbun* entitled, '*Bibimbap* Terrorism?' (9 January 2010).

6 In reference to the development of Japanese restaurants abroad, the *Asahi Shimbun* published an article stating that

worldwide Japanese cuisine has gone 'beyond a boom, moving toward a global standard' (15 January 2008).

[7] Italy and Thailand have a system of nationally authorised restaurants. In France, private organisations give seals of recommendation for French cooking.

[8] Until 1962, Korea followed the Japanese model of protecting cultural properties. However, with the enactment of the Korean Law for the Protection of Cultural Properties in 1962, the system was revised and developed along independent lines (Ôhashi 2004).

[9] A Pimatgol bar with a 65 year history was reportedly moved to the Seoul History Museum (*Joong Ang Daily*, 5 February 2010).

[10] The Olympics and the World Exposition set off this rapid economic expansion. Japan held the Olympics in 1964 and the World Expo at Osaka in 1970. The Olympics were held in Korea in 1988, and the Taejon Expo took place in 1993.

[11] In a Japanese–Korean dictionary, the word *mono* brings up words meaning thing, object, and stuff, but these do not convey the other meanings of *mono* that appear under Japanese dictionary definitions of the word, including matter, word, reason, and spirit. In Japanese there is also a difference between *mono* when written in *hiragana* and when written in Chinese characters. This has been discussed as follows. Abito Itô has raised the issue of the difference between *mono* when written in *hiragana* and when written in Chinese characters (see Asakura 2003: 3–4).

[12] 'Tradition' refers to history and things from the past, but it is 'a past that has been selected' or 'a history with significance' for contemporary society. For a further discussion of traditional culture in Korean society, see my essay 'Gendai Kankoku shakai ni okeru "dentô bunka" no kenkyû no gendai to tenbô' (Asakura 1992).

References

An, H 2007 *Culinary Researcher Hwang Hye-Seong*. Seoul: Namusup.

Asakura, T 1992 Gendai Kankoku Shakai Ni Okeru "Dentô Bunka" No Kenkyû No Genjô To Tenbô (The Current Status and Prospect of the Research on "Traditional Cultures" in Modern Korean Society). *Kokuritsu Minzokugaku Hakubutsukan Kenkyû Hôkoku (Bulletin of the National Museum of Ethnology)*, 17 (4): 809–851.

Asakura, T 2003 Hajime Ni (Introduction). In: Asakura, T (ed.) *Mono Kara Mita Chôsen Minzoku Bunka (Korean Ethnological Culture Seen from Objects)*. Tokyo: Shinkansha. pp. 3–5.

Asakura, T 2009 Ekkyôsuru kimchi (Kimchi That Crosses Borders). In: Shoji, H (ed.) *Imin To Tomoni Kawaru Chîki to Kokka (The Locality and the Nation That Change with Immigrants)*. Kokuritsu Minzokugaku Hakubutsukan Chôsa Hôkoku (Senri Ethnological Reports), 83: 59–67.

Hwang, H and Ishige, N 1988 *Kankoku No Shoku (Food in Korea)*. Tokyo: Heibonsha.

Itô, A 2003 Kankoku De "Mono O Tôshite-Miru" Koto (What One Sees through Objects in Korea). In: Asakura, T. (ed.) *Mono Kara Mita Chôsen Minzoku Bunka (Korean Ethnological Culture Seen from Objects)*. Tokyo: Shinkansha. pp. 11–24.

Koreana (ed.) 1997 *Tokushû: Gendai Ni Ikizuku Kankoku No Bunka Isan (Cultural Heritage That Lives in Present Society in Korea)*, 10 (1).

Moon, O 2009 Dining Elegance and Authenticity: Archaeology of Royal Court Cuisine in Korea. *Chinese and Northeast Asian Cuisines: Local, National, and Global Foodways Proceedings*. In: The 11th Symposium on Chinese Dietary Culture / 2009 ICCS International Symposium, CAPAS, Academia Sinica, Seoul, Korea, 12–14 October 2009.

Munhwajae Ch'ŏng (Cultural Properties Administration) 2009 *Statistical Data on Intangible Cultural Properties*. Seoul: Munhwajae Ch'ŏng.

Ôhashi, T 2004 Kankoku Ni Okeru Bunkazai Hôgo Shisutemu No Seiritsu To Tenkai: Seikino Tadashi Chôsa (1902) Kara Kankoku Bunkazai Hôgohô Seitei (1962) Made (The Establishment and Development of the System for the Protection of

Cultural Properties in Korea: from the 1902 Survey by Sekino Tadashi to the 1962 Enactment of the Law for the Protection of Cultural Properties). In: *Sôgô Seisaku Ronsô (Shimane Journal of Policy Studies)*, 8: 173–245.

Ye, Y 1976 *Kankoku No Ningen Kokuhô (Living Treasures in South Korea)*. Tokyo: Perikansha.

Yomiuri S 2007 *Nihonshoku Restoran Ninshô: 'Tadashî Nihonshoku' No Kijun Môkezu (Authenticating Japanese Restaurants: Decided Not to Establish Standards for 'Correct Japanese Food')*. 17th March 2007.

Yomota, I 2001 *Souru No Fûkei: Kioku to Henbô (Landscapes in Seoul: Memory and Change)*. Tokyo: Iwanami Shoten.

Yu, H 2000 *Watashi No Bunka Isan Tôsa Ki (Memoirs of My Visit to Cultural Heritage Sites)*. Tokyo: Hôsei University Press.

The concept of 'cultural landscapes' in relation to the historic port town of Tomo

Kazuo Mouri
Institute of Port-Town Culture in Setouchi

Introduction

In 1992 the UNESCO World Heritage Committee adopted a new category of World Heritage, 'Cultural Landscapes', in order to recognise and protect environments that are 'illustrative of the evolution of human society and settlement over time, under the influence of the physical constraints and/or opportunities presented by their natural environment and of successive social,

How to cite this book chapter:
Mouri, K 2016 The concept of 'cultural landscapes' in relation to the historic port town of Tomo. In: Matsuda, A and Mengoni, L E (eds.) *Reconsidering Cultural Heritage in East Asia*, Pp. 121–138. London: Ubiquity Press. DOI: http://dx.doi.org/10.5334/baz.g.

economic and cultural forces, both external and internal' (UNESCO World Heritage Centre: Article 47). Following this example, in 2004 Japan revised its Law for the Protection of Cultural Properties to include the protection of *bunkateki keikan*, a term directly translated from the English 'cultural landscapes'. Although many similarities can be seen between Cultural Landscapes defined by UNESCO and *bunkateki keikan* falling under the Japanese law, there are also significant differences, which are largely due to the existence of other related categories of cultural properties in Japan.

Bearing this in mind, the present chapter examines the recent dispute regarding the proposed construction of a bridge over the bay of the historic port town of Tomo (also known as Tomonoura), in Fukuyama City, Hiroshima Prefecture. The aim of this examination is to consider how different categories of cultural properties can, or cannot, apply for the protection of cultural landscape in Tomo.

Legal structures for the protection of cultural landscapes in Japan

It would be useful to first give an overview of the Japanese legal structures relating to the protection of cultural landscapes. In Japan, the protection of cultural heritage mostly falls within the Law for the Protection of Cultural Properties, which was enacted in 1950 and has since gone through several amendments (Agency for Cultural Affairs 2001). In considering the protection of cultural landscapes, three categories of cultural properties defined in the present Law are relevant.

Bunkateki keikan

The first category to consider is *bunkateki keikan*, which literally means 'cultural landscapes'. The Law for the Protection of

Cultural Properties defines *bunkateki keikan* as 'landscapes that have evolved in association with the modes of life or livelihoods of the people and geo-cultural features of a region, and which are indispensable to understanding the lifestyles and/or livelihoods of the people of Japan' (Article 2, Item 5).

Bunkateki keikan are in part related to UNESCO's Cultural Landscapes. UNESCO's Operational Guidelines for the Implementation of the World Heritage Convention defines Cultural Landscapes as representing 'the combined works of nature and of man' (UNESCO World Heritage Centre 2013: Article 47) and sets out three categories: 1) 'clearly defined landscape designed and created intentionally by man'; 2) 'organically evolved landscape'; and 3) 'associative cultural landscape' (UNESCO World Heritage Centre 2013: Annex 3, Article 10). The Guidelines divide the second category 'organically evolved landscape' further into 'relict (or fossil) landscape', in which 'an evolutionary process came to an end at some time in the past', and 'continuing landscape', which retain 'an active social role in contemporary society closely associated with the traditional way of life, and in which the evolutionary process is still in progress'. Of these categories and sub-categories of UNESCO's Cultural Landscapes, 'continuing landscapes' and 'associative cultural landscapes' are related to Japanese *bunkateki keikan* (Table 1).

What is worthy of note here is that *bunkateki keikan* does not cover the 'landscapes of the past, where no present residents maintain the modes of life or livelihood activities' that originally contributed to their formation (Edani 2012: 3), and as such cannot include 'relict/fossil landscapes' as defined by UNESCO. This means that *bunkateki keikan*, in comparison with UNESCO's Cultural Landscapes, places greater emphasis on the continuity of activities associated with the concerned landscapes by the local population. This characteristic is also noticeable in the eight types

<table>
<tr><th colspan="2">UNESCO's Operational Guidelines for the Implementation of the World Heritage Convention (2013 version)</th><th>Related categories of Japanese cultural properties as defined in the Law for the Protection of Cultural Properties</th></tr>
<tr><td colspan="2">Clearly defined landscape designed and created intentionally by man</td><td>Mainly meishô</td></tr>
<tr><td rowspan="2">Organically evolved landscape</td><td>Relict (or fossil) landscape</td><td>Mainly meishô</td></tr>
<tr><td>Continuing landscape</td><td>Mainly bunkateki keikan, and potentially also dentôteki kenzôbutsugun hozon chiku</td></tr>
<tr><td colspan="2">Associative cultural landscape</td><td>In part bunkateki keikan, and in part meishô</td></tr>
</table>

Table 1: Relation between the categories of UNESCO's Cultural Landscape and the related categories of cultural properties in the Japanese Law for the Protection of Cultural Properties.

of *bunkateki keikan* set out by the Japanese Ministry of Education, Culture, Sports, Science and Technology:

- Places related to agriculture, such as rice paddies and farmland.
- Reed plains used for harvesting grass, and pastures used for grazing livestock.
- Forests, such as timber forests and disaster prevention forests.
- Places related to aquaculture, such as fisheries and seaweed fields.
- Places involving the use of water, such as reservoirs, waterways and ports.
- Places related to mining and industry, such as mines, quarries, and factories.

- Places related to transportation and communication, such as roads and plazas.
- Places associated with dwellings, such as fences and coppices.

(Ministry of Education, Culture, Sports, Science and Technology 2005: Notice No.47)

These eight types of place relate to primary industries involving farming, forests and water and secondary and tertiary industries closely associated with the land. Importantly, all of these industries are supposed to actively continue to date. It is interesting to note that even urban landscapes can be designated as *bunkateki keikan*, as far as there is continuity of the associated livelihoods of local people.

The process for designating *bunkateki keikan* has two stages. First, municipal governments decide on their local cultural landscapes to be protected and accordingly set out plans to safeguard them. Thereafter, at the request of the municipal governments, the Ministry of Education, Culture, Sports, Science and Technology assesses and designates these locally protected landscapes as *jûyô bunkateki keikan* (meaning 'important cultural landscape') to give them national level protection.

Meishô

Although 'relict/fossil landscapes' cannot be designated as *bunkateki keikan*, they could be protected as *meishô* as defined by the Law for the Protection of Cultural Properties. *Meishô* is closely associated with traditional Japanese concepts of appreciating places, such as *meisho*, *kyûseki* and *utamakura*, and refers in particular to places of scenic beauty. While the concept of *meishô* existed even before the establishment of the modern state of Japan and the concomitant institutionalisation of legal structures for protecting cultural properties, it was only towards the end of the Meiji period that *meishô* came to be considered under threat of destruction (Watanabe 2006: 74). During the Meiji period, Japan aimed to compete politically and economically with the Western powers, and accordingly rushed to open up land, build new roads, lay down railway lines and construct large-scale factories. The 1919 Law for the Preservation of Historical Sites, Places of Scenic Beauty and Natural Monuments was enacted as a response to this situation; the *meishô* designated by this law were given legal protection for the first time. In 1950, the 1919 Law was integrated into the newly established Law for the Protection of Cultural Properties, and *meishô* became a category of cultural properties under the group of *shiseki meishô tennenkinenbutsu* (historic sites, places of scenic beauty and natural monuments).

According to the present Law for the Protection of Cultural Properties, a place can be designated as a *meishô* if it is 'an indispensable place due to the superior beauty of its terrain' (Ministry of Education 1995: Notice No.24). This designation can cover both natural places and places related to human activities. To make the criterion for designation more precise, the Ministry of Education (1995: Notice No.24) set out eleven different types of *meishô*, which are: (1) parks and gardens; (2) bridges and embankments; (3) places with flowering trees, grasses and other foliage; (4) locations of wildlife, fish and insects; (5) rocks and caves; (6) canyons, waterfalls, mountain streams and ravines; (7) lakes, wetlands, floating islands and spring fountains; (8) dunes, sandbars, beaches and islands; (10) volcanos and hot springs; and (11) vantage points. Importantly, whether a place can be designated as a *meishô* is largely based on aesthetic judgement, which means that the livelihood of local people and their relationship to the place are not taken into consideration (Hirasawa 2009: 102–103).

Of the three categories of UNESCO's Cultural Landscapes shown earlier, *meishô* are related to 'clearly defined landscapes designed and created intentionally by man', such as gardens and parks, 'relict/fossil landscapes', and some of the 'associative cultural landscapes', especially those having religious and/or artistic associations (Table 1).

Dentôteki kenzôbutsugun hozon chiku

Another category of Japanese cultural properties that is relevant to the protection of cultural landscapes is *dentôteki kenzôbutsugun hozon chiku*, or preservation districts for groups of traditional buildings.

After the Second World War, despite the enactment of the Law for the Protection of Cultural Properties in 1950, the strategic drive towards post-war recovery by means of rapid economic growth resulted in the loss of much historic environment. Acknowledgement of the extent of this loss led in 1975 to the amendment of the Law for the Protection of Cultural Properties to form a system for protecting *dentôteki kenzôbutsugun* (groups of traditional buildings), which is still valid today.

Dentôteki kenzôbutsugun hozon chiku differs from *bunkateki keikan* in that it consists of a concentrated cluster of historic buildings, and as such cannot be applied to an area where there is no historical building and to a vast area where historic buildings exist but are dispersed and do not form an architectural cluster. For example, rice paddies and farmland cannot be designated as *dentôteki kenzôbutsugun hozon chiku*, although they may be protected as *bunkateki keikan*.

The process of designating *dentôteki kenzôbutsugun hozon chiku* is similar to that of designating *bunkateki keikan.* First, municipal governments designate their local preservation districts according to their own criteria, by-laws and management plans. Thereafter, the Ministry of Education, Culture, Sports, Science and Technology, at the request of the municipal governments, assesses and designates these local preservation districts as *jûyô dentôteki kenzôbutsugun hozon chiku* (important preservation districts for groups of traditional buildings) to give them national level protection.

The above review of the three categories of cultural properties clearly demonstrates that the idea of protecting cultural landscapes did exist in Japan, albeit with some limited extent, even before the adoption of the category *bunkateki keikan* in the Law for the Protection of Cultural Properties in 2004. This fact should be stressed, as it is sometimes overlooked because of the understanding that *bunkateki keikan* is a relatively new, imported term and concept. As seen above, there have been legal mechanisms to protect groups of historic buildings as *dentôteki kenzôbutsugun hozon chiku* since 1975, and places of scenic beauty as *meishô* since 1919. In this sense, the adoption of *bunkateki keikan* should be understood as a means to expand the coverage of protection of cultural landscapes in Japan. With this in mind, let us now examine the case of the protection of cultural landscape in Tomo.

The historic port town of Tomo

Tomo's position on the coast of Honshu facing Shikoku places it within the central area of the Seto Inland Sea (Figure 1). Until the development of the steamship, Japanese ships relied on wind and

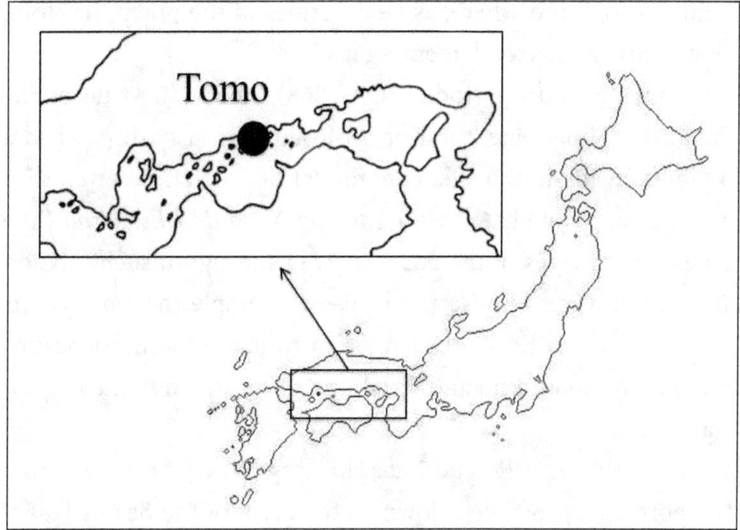

Figure 1: Tomo's location in the Japanese archipelago and the Seto Inland Sea (upper box) (map design by Akira Matsuda).

tide for power, and ports were therefore sited in places like Tomo where it was convenient to wait for the changing of the tides. Located on a small bay about 500 metres across, backed by mountains and with many islands nearby, Tomo's geographical situation was ideally suited to the commercial activity of a port town.

The historic town of Tomo that we see today came into being during the first half of the 19th-century, although its origins go back much earlier. The town appears in the *Man'yôshû* (Collection of Ten Thousand Leaves), an official poetry collection compiled during the 8th-century, when the ancient Japanese state was consolidated. The author of one poem (Book 3, 0446) was a courtier appointed to set up a diplomatic post in a province of Kyushu, the southern gateway to Japan. He and his wife travelled there together, visiting Tomo on the way. The courtier's wife died during his tenure, however, and on the journey back to the capital he returned to Tomo where, as he describes in the poem, he stood alone staring at a tree, lamenting his loss.

During the Edo period (1603–1868), under the rule of the Tokugawa Shogunate, the Korean Joseon Dynasty dispatched a diplomatic mission to offer congratulations each time a new shogun was appointed. According to the *Nittô daiichi keishô* (The Finest Landscapes of the East), in 1711 the eighth such mission stopped at a guesthouse in an historic temple in Tomo on its journey back to Korea. When asked to name the most beautiful place between Edo and Tsushima, the mission replied that it was Tomo.

During the same Edo period a shipping route was opened from the northeast provinces, down to the coast of the Sea of Japan/East Sea, and then via the Seto Inland Sea up to Osaka. *Kitamae-bune,* north-bound ships, transported goods along the route and trade grew. As the Japanese economy prospered, Tomo flourished, reaching a peak in the mid-19th-century. Today, Tomo is the only place in Japan that maintains a complete set of the five fixtures that a port needed in order to function during the Edo period (The Sixth Subcommittee of the Japan ICOMOS 2007: 1–4): *jôy-atô* (a large lantern on a high stand serving as a lighthouse); *gangi* (a stepped embankment where a ship could be hauled out of the sea and drained of seawater); *funabansho* (a marine warden's office); *namidome* (a breakwater); and *tateba* (a dry dock for ship maintenance).

Contemporary society may recognise Tomo as the hometown of the anime character Ponyo, known to many through the movie *Ponyo on the Cliff by the Sea* (*Gake no ue no Ponyo*) produced in 2008 by the internationally renowned film director Hayao Miyazaki. Tomo shaped Ponyo's conception, and various sites in the town appeared in scenes throughout the film, including streets and neighbourhoods built during the Edo period, which contributed to the rise of popularity of Tomo's landscape nationwide.

Certain aspects of Tomo's landscape have been under legal protection for several decades. In 1925, the small islands near the port that have traditionally been the subject of aesthetic appreciation to be viewed from Tomo were designated as a *meishô* under the 1919 law, and in 1934, a wide area of the Seto Inland Sea was designated as a national park, under the name of Setonaikai National Park. Both designations are still valid today. In addition, in 2008 Fukuyama City designated an 8.6 hectare (21.25 acre) area of the historic quarter of Tomo as a *dentôteki kenzôbutsugun hozon chiku* (preservation district for groups of traditional buildings). The area incorporates 102 buildings from the Edo period, 85 buildings from the Meiji period (1868–1912) and 270 traditional buildings constructed before the Second World War (Mouri 2011: 5). It is important to note that this designation protects a particular cluster of buildings without taking a broader view of their geographical context, and thus excludes some of the key port facilities. As of spring 2015, this *dentôteki kenzôbutsugun hozon chiku* still remains a local designation and has yet to receive national level protection.

Dispute regarding the plans to build a traffic bridge on reclaimed land at Tomo

Traffic flow in Tomo has long been a critical issue in relation to both economic development and historic preservation. Since the main road was only four meters wide (Figure 2), large vehicles were not able to drive there and even smaller cars were dangerously close when they passed. In 1983, Hiroshima Prefectural Government put forward plans to alleviate the problem

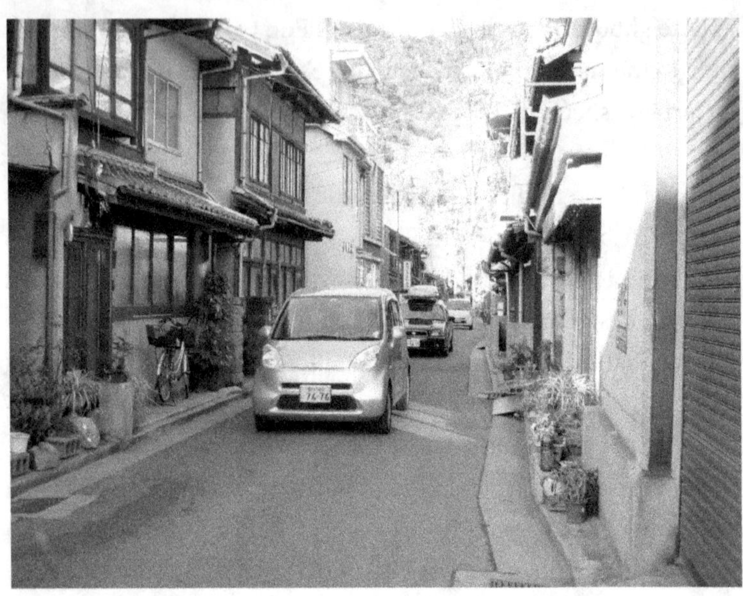

Figure 2: The main road in Tomo, which is only about four metres wide (photo by Akira Matsuda)

by constructing a bridge on reclaimed land in the historic port. While the bridge was intended primarily to improve the living conditions of local residents, rather than to achieve large-scale economic development, the impact of its construction became a focus for the endemic tension between the town's economic growth and historic preservation, highlighting the difficulty of operating within the legislative framework for the protection of Tomo's unique cultural landscape. If construction of the bridge had gone ahead, large vehicles that until then had been unable to enter Tomo would have been routed through the town, inevitably affecting its historic landscape and potentially endangering its residents. A number of local residents protested against the plans and initiated a lawsuit demanding that permission for land reclamation be denied on the basis that it would compromise the scenery of the port.

In the lawsuit, the plaintiffs, residents of Tomo, claimed that the whole environment of Tomo measuring 1,779 ha (4,396 acres) should be carefully taken into consideration in town planning, and special attention should be paid to the landscape of the historic centre, including the historic port (43 ha or 106.3 acres) and the combined district of historic streets and buildings, temples and shrines (35 ha or 86.5 acres). These residents argued that no approval should be given for works that would significantly detract from this landscape (Mouri 2011: 5).

In response, the defendant, Hiroshima Prefectural Government, claimed that there was no problem with the works as long as they were not carried out in the area designated as a *meishô* according to the Law for the Protection of Cultural Properties. Here it should be remembered that this *meishô* area does not include the port area but only the small islands surrounding Tomo. Hiroshima Prefectural Government also argued that the project would not infringe on any regulations for the management of the Setonaikai National Park, which includes Tomo and its surrounding sea but gives them only the weakest level of protection. On this basis, Hiroshima Prefectural Government maintained that the reclamation and construction project should go ahead because it would not affect the historical neighbourhoods and 'five fixtures' of the port, thus showing enough care for the preservation of cultural heritage within the proposed project.

The lawsuit, which attracted nationwide interest, resulted in a historic outcome. On October 1, 2009 the Hiroshima District Court found in favour of the plaintiffs and blocked permission for the Hiroshima Prefectural Government to proceed with the project (Mouri 2011: 5). For the first time ever in Japan, the courts refused to grant a public works permit on the grounds that the works would damage an historic landscape. The ruling concluded that Tomo's scenery has historical and cultural value and serves the public good. The official verdict stated:

> 'Tomo Port offers a splendid view of the peaceful waters of the Inland Sea and the islands floating within it. This view along with the scenery of the port itself – that is to say, its crescent-shaped coastline, its breakwaters jutting out into the sea, its stepped piers built along the quays, its night-lights lingering in the middle of the port, the remains of its ship guard station on the hill ... in combination with old streets and neighbourhoods and buildings associated with historical events – as a whole forms a beautiful scenery ... The port facilities... and the old streets, neighbourhoods and buildings tell the story of Tomo, which flourished for many years as a port town and have been the stage of historical events and of the economic, political and cultural activities of a great many people. From this point of view, it can be argued that the above-mentioned scenery is not merely valuable for its beautiful townscape but has historical and cultural value in its entirety as well'.

Although the verdict did not use the term 'cultural landscape', many aspects of it were in agreement with the concept of a 'Cultural Landscape' as defined by UNESCO, and in particular, its category of 'continuing landscape'.

Hiroshima Prefectural Government objected to the court decision and submitted an appeal. However, in June 2012, Mr Yuzaki Hidehiko, Governor of Hiroshima Prefecture elected in November 2009, announced the withdrawal of the 30-year-old plans for the construction of a bridge and instead proposed to dig a tunnel through the mountains behind the town and introduce a park-and-ride policy to alleviate the traffic problem. By stopping cars from entering the town, the Governor argued, the change in town planning policy would provide safer traffic and better living conditions for residents whilst also protecting the historic landscape. This new proposal has, however, yet to be officially accepted at the time of writing (spring 2015) due to the opposition of certain stakeholders and the concerns about the implications of the new construction work to be entailed.

While the ruling of the Hiroshima District Court and the subsequent decision by Governor Yuzaki to withdraw the plans to construct a bridge on reclaimed land was ground-breaking and suggested that the protection of cultural landscape would become a more important agenda in town planning in Japan, it also marked the beginning of a new challenge in Tomo, which was to ensure long-term protection of the town's historic landscape.

As of spring 2015, Fukuyama City does not consider the option of protecting Tomo's port landscape with the designation of *bunkateki keikan*. This seems largely due to the foreseeable great challenge of obtaining agreement from all the stakeholders, in particular those whose land use would be restricted by such designation. The possibility of the designation of *bunkateki keikan* itself will, however, remain as an option to be taken in the future.

A less difficult option, at least in theory, would be to raise the current local designation of *dentôteki kenzôbutsugun hozon chiku* (preservation district for groups of traditional buildings) to the national level designation of *jûyô dentôteki kenzôbutsugun hozon chiku* (important preservation district for groups of traditional buildings). As already stated, however, this has not materialised to date, despite Fukuyama City's intention to achieve it sooner.

One reason of the delay is that the national Agency for Cultural Affairs, which reports to the Ministry of Education, Culture, Sports, Science and Technology, is not convinced yet whether the area for protection currently set in the local designation is adequate. In 2010, the Agency for Cultural Affairs advised Fukuyama City to examine whether the designated area was not too small, and Fukuyama City has since been working on it, considering whether or not to include the ancient zone that houses historic temples and shrines (*teramachi*). What makes the situation complicated, however, is that the local designation had been made on the assumption that the bridge over the bay would eventually be constructed. With the bridge construction suspended indefinitely, the residents of the historical quarter have been left uncertain as to whether their living conditions could be brought up to the standards of modern society under the even tighter national level protection.

Conclusion

In Japan, certain forms of cultural landscape were protected as *meishô* and *dentôteki kenzôbutsugun hozon chiku* already before the adoption of the category *bunkateki keikan* in the Law for the Protection of Cultural Properties in 2004. The adoption of *bunkateki keikan*, however, contributed to the expansion of the scope of protection of cultural landscape, and as a result the landscapes that have developed in close association with the modes of life and livelihood of the local population came under legal protection.

Against this background of increased interest in the protection of cultural landscapes nationwide, the Hiroshima District Court ruled against the construction of a bridge over the bay of Tomo's port in October 2009, on the grounds that the town's historic landscape was valuable as a public good and therefore deserved protection. This ground-breaking ruling led Hiroshima Prefecture Government to suspend the construction of the bridge indefinitely, and Tomo has since been tackling the new challenge to find an appropriate mechanism for the long-term protection of its port landscape. Elevating the currently local designation of *dentôteki kenzôbutsugun hozon chiku* to the national level designation would probably be the first task in this challenge. Considering the need to safeguard the wider port landscape as well as to achieve sustainable development in the town, designating the Tomo's whole historic landscape associated with local people's livelihood as a *bunkateki keikan* might be necessary in the long term.

References

Agency for Cultural Affairs 2001 *Bunkazai Hogohô Gojûnenshi* (*The Fifty Year Old History of the Law for the Protection of Cultural Properties*). Tokyo: Gyosei.

Edani, H 2012 Conservation and Management of Cultural Landscapes. Nara National Research Institute for Cultural Properties. http://www.nara.accu.or.jp/elearning/2012/conservation.pdf (accessed on 1 September 2015).

Hirasawa, T 2009 Bunkazai To Shiteno Bunkateki Keikan No Haaku Rikai Hyôka No Tameno Shiten To Chôsa Kenkyû No Hôkôsei Ni Tsuite (Perspectives for the Understanding and Evaluation of Cultural Landscapes as Cultural Properties and the Direction of Future Research). In: *Bunkateki Keikan Kenkyû Syûkai Daiikkai Hôkokusyo (Report from the First Research Conference on Cultural Landscapes)*. Nara: Nara National Research Institute for Cultural Properties. pp. 96–122.

Mitchell, N, Rössler, M and Tricaud, P (eds.) 2009 *World Heritage Cultural Landscapes: A Handbook for Conservation and Management.* Paris: UNESCO.

Mouri, K 2011 Ryôkôna Keikan No Keisei To Kankôryoku (Formulation of Good Landscape and Tourism Power). *The Archaeological Journal (Kôkogaku Jânaru)*, 609: 4–8.

The Sixth Subcommittee of the Japan ICOMOS 2007 *Rekishiteki Kôwan Toshi 'Tomo No Ura': Bunkaisan Hogo Ni Kakawaru Chôsa Kenkyû Hôkokusho* (Historical Port Town 'Tomo no ura': Research Report for the Protection of its Cultural Heritage), http:www.japan-icomos.org/workgroup06/1stICOMOSReportText.pdf (accessed on 1 September 2015).

UNESCO World Heritage Centre 2013 *Operational Guidelines for the Implementation of the World Heritage Convention*. http://whc.unesco.org/archive/opguide13-en.pdf (accessed on 1 September 2015).

Watanabe, A 2006 *The Japanese System for Safeguarding Cultural Heritage*. In: UNESCO (ed.) *Proceedings of the International Conference on the Safeguarding of Tangible and Intangible Cultural Heritage: Towards an Integrated Approach*. UNESCO, Paris: UNESCO. pp. 74–97.

Shaping Japan's disaster heritage

The creation of new monuments and the preservation of ruins in the aftermath of the Great East Japan Earthquake and Tsunami

Megan Good
Independent researcher

Introduction

Through the examination of major volcanic eruptions, Sheets and Grayson (1979) were among the first to suggest that the cultural evolution of a society may be directly influenced by the catastrophic natural disasters it experiences. This theory has since been expanded upon by various heritage professionals examining how all types of natural disasters, such as earthquakes, tsunamis, landslides, and hurricanes, have the potential for long-term impact on the lives of those affected and the society as a whole

How to cite this book chapter:
Good, M 2016 Shaping Japan's disaster heritage. In: Matsuda, A and Mengoni, L E (eds.) *Reconsidering Cultural Heritage in East Asia*, Pp. 139–161. London: Ubiquity Press. DOI: http://dx.doi.org/10.5334/baz.h.

(Kornbacher 2002; Oliver-Smith 1986; Sheets & Grayson 1979: 628). As noted by Oliver-Smith (1996: 303), natural disasters 'signal the failure of a society to adapt successfully to certain features of its natural and socially constructed environment in a sustainable fashion', and, in this way, highlight the limits of a society's adaptive processes. If this is truly the case then, according to Torrence and Grattan (2002), it follows that studying the ways in which a society responds to disasters would be an important avenue to understanding the broader processes of that society's historical and cultural evolution. One way in which to study these responses is to examine particular aspects of a society's cultural heritage thought to have emerged as a direct result of a disaster.

Monuments commemorating tsunami disasters have existed in Japan for centuries in the form of *tsunamihi* – a term derived from a combination of the word '*tsunami*', meaning a very large ocean wave caused by an underwater earthquake or volcanic eruption, and '*hi*', meaning a stone monument with an inscription. *Tsunamihi* are large stone tablets or elongated rocks ranging from three to even ten feet tall, set into the ground and featuring inscriptions. When the recent Great East Japan Earthquake and Tsunami struck on March 11, 2011, some residents turned to these monuments for guidance on where to find safe ground, and recalled the messages inscribed on their surface which contain warnings from their ancestors of the dangers of earthquakes and their ensuing tsunami. The earliest known *tsunamihi* date as far back as the 14th-century (Murakami 2008). These traditional stone monuments represent a part of Japan's unique heritage – its 'disaster heritage'. More recently, however, Japan began seeing a new form of memorialising tsunami disasters, which involves the preservation of ruins.

Prior to the Meiji period (1868–1912), most of Japan's infrastructure was made of wood. When a disaster struck, the wood would burn away or topple over into unrecognisable debris. Western-style masonry was not introduced into Japan until around the beginning of the Meiji period. For many European observers Japan's lack of significant masonry ruins was seen as contributing to a certain 'absence of memory', in contrast to European nations where stone ruins provided a clear and constant reminder of the past (Weisenfeld 2012: 150). Since that time, there have been a few cases in which materials damaged by earthquakes have been preserved; for example, at the Kanto Earthquake Memorial Museum and the Nojima Fault Preservation Museum, which commemorate the Great Kanto Earthquake of 1923 and the Hanshin-Awaji Earthquake of 1995, respectively.

Since the March 11, 2011 disaster (from hereon referred to simply as 3.11), there have been debates in the affected communities up and down the affected coast about how best to commemorate the disaster and, for the first time, a significant number of proposals have been put forth by local governments, citizens, and scholars for various ruins of the tsunami to be preserved as either monuments that stand on their own or as part of a memorial park. Among the proposals were, for instance, three damaged concrete buildings in the town of Onagawa (Figure 1), a lone surviving pine tree (one of 70,000 before the disaster), a message on the wall of a community centre in Rikuzentakata city, a tour bus stranded on top of a building in the city of Ishinomaki, and a 330-ton fishing boat washed ashore in Kesennuma city.

Bearing these in mind, this chapter investigates the relationship between natural disasters and the evolution of cultural practices by focusing on Japan's long history of destructive tsunamis and the monuments built by generations past and present to commemorate them. Through comparison with Japan's traditional *tsunamihi*, it attempts to understand why after 3.11 the newer

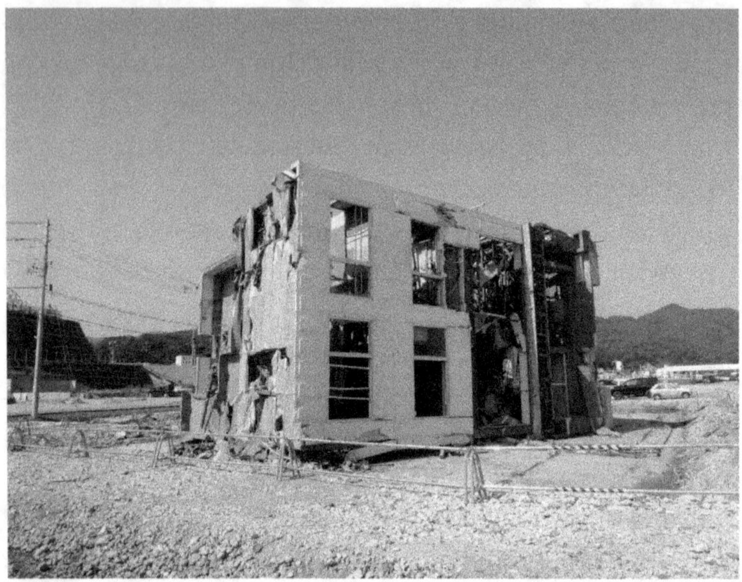

Figure 1: One of the three damaged buildings left *in situ* in Onagawa Town (photographed in July 2012 by Akira Matsuda). This building was subsequently dismantled and removed in January 2015.

notion of preserving ruins of the tsunami became so popular and yet so controversial.

Japan's ancestral stone monuments: *tsunamihi*

The 3.11 earthquake occurred at precisely 14:46 JST off the coast of north-east Honshu, the main island of Japan, measuring in at a magnitude of 9.0 on Richeter scale. The resulting tsunami was 8 to 9 m high and reached an upstream height of 40 m, leaving an estimated 19,500 people either dead or missing (Japan ICOMOS National Committee 2011: iii). Although described in the media as 'unprecedented', 3.11 was not the first event of its kind to ravage

Tôhoku, the north-eastern region of Honshu. Earthquakes measuring greater than M8.0 triggered catastrophic tsunamis along the eastern coast of the Tôhoku region killing thousands in 869, 1611, 1896, and 1933. The 1896 tsunami incurred the highest loss of life by a tsunami ever recorded in Japanese history at an estimated 22,000 lives lost (National Geographical Data Center n.d.); however the 3.11 tsunami was a close second.

In the wake of 3.11, while some praised the advanced earthquake resistant buildings that undoubtedly saved countless lives in cities like Tokyo, others focused more on the inherited memories of past tsunamis that saved many in rural towns across Tôhoku. This included oral traditions such as those in Murohama, located in Miyato Island in the city of Higashi Matsushima, where over the years local people had passed down stories about the two tsunami waves that devastated the island during the Jôgan tsunami of 869:

> 'A millennium ago, the residents of Murohama, knowing they were going to be inundated, had sought safety on the village's closest hill. But they had entered into a deadly trap. A second wave, which had reached the interior of the island through an inlet, was speeding over the rice paddies from the opposite direction. The waves collided at the hill and killed those who had taken refuge there. To signify their grief and to advise future generations, the survivors erected a shrine' (Holguín-Veras 2012).

Inherited memory of how the tsunami had behaved in 869 meant that people understood what to do, and what not to do, when the earthquake struck on 3.11 – despite the failure of the Murohama tsunami-warning tower to sound the alarm (Holguín-Veras 2012).

A clear example of the value of *tsunamihi* during 3.11 comes from the small town of Aneyoshi, Iwate Prefecture. Residents cited as their saving grace a *tsunamihi* that remained from their ancestors who experienced the devastating 1896 tsunami. The message on the stone monument warns people not to build their homes below the place it marks. Heeding this warning, the village was safe on high ground when the 3.11 tsunami struck (Fackler 2011).[1] Hundreds of these *tsunamihi* dot the east coast of Japan with inscriptions ranging from religious sutras (in the case of the very old *tsunamihi*), detailed accounts of the disaster (e.g. lives lost, houses destroyed, height of the tsunami, and its behaviours), to simple instructive messages such as 'if there is an earthquake, think only of yourself and run to high ground'.

The inscriptions on *tsunamihi* provide some reflection of the nature of society's changing beliefs over time concerning the underlying causes of tsunamis and their control over their own fate when they occurred. For example, early producers of *tsunamihi,* such as those who created Kôryakuhi, the oldest known *tsunamihi*, built in 1380 in the town of Minami in Tokushima Prefecture, appear to have done so for religious purposes. The sutra engraved on the surface of Kôryakuhi is testament to the Buddhist beliefs of the community at the time. It was believed that natural disasters were a punishment for those who did not live righteously according to Buddhist Law (Asma 2011), and blame was often placed on the victims of the disaster.[2] The same sutra can also be found on later *tsunamihi,* including one commemorating the tsunami which struck Tokushima Prefecture in 1605 (Murakami 2008). This 1605 *tsunamihi* not only bears this Buddhist element, but juxtaposes it with a small shrine for a Shinto deity which is indicative of the rise of Shintoism in the region during the Edo period (1603–1867) (Murakami 2008). Whereas under Buddhist teachings earthquakes had been associated with karmic retribution, Shinto taught that earthquakes and tsunamis were the result of the god Kashima's negligence.

According to Shinto folklore, *namazu*, a giant catfish, lives in the bowels of the Earth and is restrained by a large stone held in place by the god Kashima. Sometimes Kashima gets distracted with other business and *namazu* gets free and thrashes about violently, causing earthquakes to occur (Smits 2006). Under these circumstances, blame is placed with the negligence of a god, not with any moral failures of society associated with Buddhist values. During the Edo period, inscriptions on *tsunamihi* began to include, alongside religious elements, a record documenting the date, time, location, and sometimes behaviour of the tsunami. It was also during this period that literacy became more widespread (Deal 2006), giving more people the chance to read and learn about the tsunami event from the stone monuments.[3] It was perhaps then during this period that people may have begun to feel that they had some control over what would happen to them when a disaster struck, particularly if they knew what they should be prepared for.

By the start of the Meiji period, modern scientific explanations began to undermine any lingering literal beliefs in *namazu* causing earthquakes (Smits 2006). The emergence of seismology and a growing interest in the study of historical earthquakes in Japan – by Japanese as well as foreign scholars, including Fusakichi Ômori, Ichizô Hattori, Sekiya Seikei, John Milne, Thomas Gray, John Perry, and Edmond Naumann – provided the main catalyst for this shift.[4] By the time the 1896 tsunami struck, stone monuments exhibiting purely educational inscriptions were emerging, such as the one in Aneyoshi mentioned previously. When the 1933 tsunami occurred, many people who had experienced the 1896 tsunami were still alive. Also, during this time seismologists were publishing, for the first time, research that hinted at a historical trend in Japan's earthquakes. Together these factors led to the realisation among scholars, as well as residents affected by the 1933 disaster, that other massive earthquake and tsunami events were an inevitable part of Japan's future. As a result, stone monuments exhibiting messages related to disaster prevention, such as warnings and safety instructions, became more numerous and widespread. In Miyagi Prefecture alone, approximately seven *tsunamihi* were erected in various places after the 1896 tsunami, and at least forty emerged along the coast following the 1933 disaster (Institute of Disaster Mitigation for Urban Cultural Heritage 2012).

After 3.11, the National General Association for Stone Shops in Japan began to erect 500 coastal stone monuments very similar to past *tsunamihi* but modernised to include English translation and QR (Quick Response) codes linking to images and video of the disaster (Weitzman 2011). Like their most recent forebears these *tsunamihi* serve educational purposes to teach about the dangers of earthquake and tsunami events.

The history of Japan's *tsunamihi* tells us that communities erect monuments to tsunami disasters for at least three distinct reasons: prayer, education, and healing. Although *tsunamihi* no longer have religious elements in their inscriptions, they still carry a spiritual meaning for some. Savage (2006) suggests that heritage, inclusive of monuments, provides a 'technology' for healing. Similar to a grave stone, the erection of a memorial monument can serve as a systematic way of progressing through the grieving process for victims who lost loved ones, homes, and livelihoods to the disaster. It is important to note that *tsunamihi* are made from new material and as such can symbolise a new beginning for a community devastated by the disaster and provide a means of educating, via the messages inscribed on their surface, without evoking emotional stress from victims.

Preventing memories from fading

Despite the unprecedented number of 3.11 *tsunamihi* being erected along the affected coastal areas, there have been voices inside and outside the devastated communities for many of the ruins resulting from the tsunami to be preserved. This is a significant phenomenon, considering that such ruins may well evoke painful memories of the disaster for their victims. Those who are in favour of preserving the ruins of the disaster as monuments seem to think that the ruins are useful in ways that *tsunamihi* are not.

One explanation for the push toward preserving the ruins as monuments may be that the traditional *tsunamihi* are not effective enough in educating people about the need to prepare for the tsunami to come. As stated, one of the aims of *tsunamihi* since the Edo period has been to pass on the memory of the terrible event, so that the suffering experienced by one generation will not be experienced by future generations. In reality, however, people have often forgotten the terror of tsunami with the passing of time. In the aftermath of 3.11, for example, many of the affected communities (with Aneyoshi as one of the only exceptions) were criticised for having built their homes in areas known to have been devastated by previous tsunamis, and with the knowledge that another one was sure to come. Despite the knowledge passed down through the *tsunamihi* revealing the inundation points of past tsunami – thus indicating where homes might be safe to build – memories faded and people ignored them.

The inability of the *tsunamihi* to keep people aware of the terror of tsunami may provide one reason why people want the ruins of 3.11 to be preserved as monuments. They perhaps feel that, unlike *tsunamihi*, ruins could conjure this feeling, as Weisenfeld (2012: 139–140) explains:

> 'The aesthetics of catastrophe inevitably stimulate our senses while evoking our emotions and empathy. The imaging of disaster does not allow the viewer to remain dispassionate about the tragedy of an earthquake or ignore its ocular dimensions'.

Similarly, Petzet (2003) argues that monuments do not consist of physical properties alone but that they also convey an 'aura' or 'feeling value', which is 'present *in situ* even when they no longer exist or are hardly comprehensible as 'historic fabric' (Petzet 2003: 2). Advocates of preserving the 3.11 tsunami ruins seem to hope that this feeling value has more power to instil the dangers of a tsunami than just the knowledge itself.

One could also argue that material preservation provides a sense of continuity with the past; a direct link with the event that new monuments cannot provide (Lowenthal 1989). In this way, monumentalising ruins of the disaster could be considered as society's next logical step up from *tsunamihi* in the desperate attempt to solidify collective emotional memory of the event, so that future generations do not forget and make the same mistakes.

The controversial cases of Rikuzentakata and Onagawa

The following two proposals for the preservation of materials damaged by the 3.11 tsunami demonstrate how two communities have attempted to solidify collective memory in their communities and the controversy that followed. These case studies illustrate the problematic in attempting to achieve a universal solution to the debate concerning the preservation of the ruins of the tsunami rather than a case-by-case assessment.

In the aftermath of 3.11, roughly 10,000 people were living in 80 evacuation shelters in the coastal city of Rikuzentakata. In April 2012, several months after the tsunami devastated the town, a message appeared on a wall in the town's damaged community centre which adjoined a gymnasium. The message was written by two sisters whose mother was an employee at the community centre and a victim who died taking refuge there when the tsunami came (Figure 2). It reads:

> Dear Mom,
> Thank you so much for everything.
> You always come to me in my dreams and are kind.
> Your smile is always kind
> And there is no doubt that you are a great mom.
> Even if the gymnasium is taken down,
> I absolutely will not forget this place.
> Really, thank you mom.
> My mom who I love so much,
> Protect and watch over our family from heaven, ok?
> Because from now on I will do my best!

The message had an unexpected echo inside and outside the community. Dr Makoto Manabe, a specialist in vertebrate palaeontology at the National Museum of Nature and Science, helped gather a petition of 1,723 signatures to preserve the message as a monument to the disaster. Dr Manabe argued that the message has the power to help alleviate the pain of surviving victims by reminding them of the good memories of those they lost, such as the kind smile of the mother the message is addressed to, and it also encourages others going through the hardship of rebuilding their lives to 'do [their] best' (Makoto Manabe 2012, personal

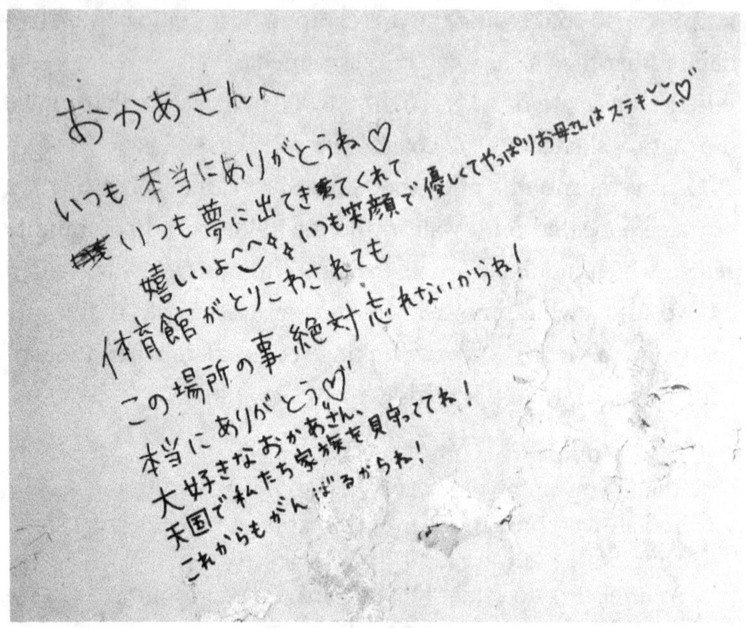

Figure 2: Message left on a wall of a community centre in Rikuzentakata city (photo by Akira Matsuda).

communication, 9 June). He raised the point that many people can connect to the love of a family member as portrayed in the contents of the message (Tohkai Shimpo 2012b).

The case to physically preserve the message is much more complex, however, than saying its preservation would be beneficial to victims. The city would have to consider how to acquire funds for its preservation, whether the entire building or the wall only should be preserved, and whether the money could be better used on something else. Mayor Futoshi Toba of Rikuzentakata had his priorities set on first building a 40-foot sea wall before concentrating on a memorial park (Craft 2012), but was swayed by the petition to preserve the message by cutting it out of the wall of the community centre and storing it in an old school until the method of display could be agreed upon. Mayor Toba addressed the decision by saying the message would serve as testament to the tsunami's impact on affected residents and pass that truth on to future generations. Preserving the message cost around 2 million yen (US$20,000) taken from the city's budget (Tohkai Shimpo 2012a). This case raises the question: who has the right to decide if and in what form a monument should be built?

A little south of Rikuzentakata is the small port town of Onagawa on the northeast coast of Miyagi Prefecture. Mayor Nobutaka Azumi was worried that people would not want to return and live again in Onagawa and, therefore, wanted to ensure the town recovered quickly. Only two months after the disaster, Onagawa became one of the first towns affected by the tsunami to map out a reconstruction plan (*Onagawa Town Reconstruction Development Committee* 2011). The proposed plan called for a memorial park in which three damaged buildings would be preserved as monuments. In their damaged state it was seen that these buildings would serve to remind people of the destructive capabilities of a tsunami. Additionally, the memorial park would cover much of the town area vulnerable to future tsunamis, thereby preventing current and future residents from building their homes and businesses in this dangerous zone.

After a few more months, many of the town's elders began to fight against Mayor Azumi's proposals, arguing that they wanted the ancestral villages rebuilt so that they could spend their remaining years there, despite knowing they would be vulnerable to future tsunamis. In Onagawa, the average age of residents is around fifty, and their majority vote appears to be over-ruling the younger generations who support plans for reconstruction based on establishing more long-term sustainable communities. Mayor Azumi was soon pushed out of office by Yoshiaki Suda, who supported the elder populations wishes (Onishi 2012). Due to the strong differing opinions of the residents, a final decision on whether to preserve the buildings or not was not immediately forthcoming.[5] Many residents, particularly younger residents and school children, likened the importance of the preservation of the buildings to the Hiroshima Atomic Bomb Dome, which took twenty years to reach a decision to preserve (Japan Broadcasting Corporation [NHK] 2013a).

There are other issues that leaders in the affected communities must consider besides differences of opinions about the form commemoration should take. For instance, in creating memorial parks both Onagawa and Rikuzentakata would have to create new space for the project and deal with land ownership issues. With a limited amount of funds available to aid in the reconstruction efforts, some local officials find it difficult justifying spending money on monuments when it could be going towards new homes, food, schools, psychological aid for victims, and/or other avenues that are arguably of greater priority.

The message on the wall in Rikuzentakata is similar to *tsunamihi* in that the aura and message itself commemorates the disaster, while also encouraging people to look to the future. Conversely, the buildings in Onagawa draw the people's attention to the past and do not attempt to convey any encouragement for the future or comfort for the victims. Those proposing the preservation of 3.11 ruins as monuments face the difficult task of not only considering current residents, but also envisaging how the monuments will be perceived by future generations, as well as by tourists. Reconciliation of all stakeholders' wishes appears to be impossible. Not only will various stakeholders have different and often polarized opinions, there will also be other considerations, such as access to funds, space, and other resources necessary for the monument to become a reality. Consequently, decisions must be made that will inevitably favour certain opinions and priorities over others.

Constructing disaster tourism

Picture the following scene in a park: it is daytime and the sky is a clear blue with only a few puffy white clouds. The grass and trees appear a brilliant green. At the centre of this scene the ruins of the Onagawa Police Box sit preserved in a see-through glass case for visitors to the park to look upon. A nearby sign post presumably describes this concrete building as one of very few able to withstand the massive tsunami that swept through the town of Onagawa on March 11, 2011 killing over 800 residents and displacing approximately 5,700 others. Families, couples, and tourists are happily walking about in their summer clothes as they point and smile at the exhibit before them. In the foreground a man poses for a picture as he stands smiling and pointing at the encased ruin behind him.

This scene is derived straight from the Onagawa Reconstruction Plan published in 2011, which is available on the town's website (Onagawa Town Reconstruction Development Committee 2011). The visitors in the illustration appear to be *enjoying* the ruin. Setting the scene in this way suggests an attempt to convey the town's success in overcoming the damage and grief caused by the disaster – people smiling as if they are no longer suffering from the after-effects and green foliage indicative of healthy new life and vitality in the disaster-affected area. Thus, it encourages the stance that the preservation of the ruined Onagawa Police Box is a positive development for the community, one that the Onagawa Reconstruction Plan assures will help pass on the memory and lessons of the disaster to future generations and pay tribute to its victims. It also highlights another driving factor for preserving these ruins: tourism. One may wonder, though, whether this scene is not a little unsettling.

In his 2004 article 'A Terrible Beauty', Mark Dery asks the following question: 'Does our humanity falter if we acknowledge an esthetic sublime in the visual facade of tragedy?'. He goes on to remark on 'the moral vertigo we feel when we gaze, rapt, at images of spectacular tragedies and simulated horrors, viewing the real and recreational alike through esthetic eyes' (in Weisenfeld 2012: 139). Sites of death and disaster attract millions of visitors worldwide including Auschwitz-Birkenau, Anne Frank's House, the Hiroshima Atomic Bomb Dome, Pompeii, and Chernobyl, so there is reason to believe the tsunami ruins will also entice visitors. In October 2013, the NHK reported that in Fukushima Prefecture alone there had been 23 tours involving five hundred participants in which groups led by local residents who had experienced the disaster toured the nuclear evacuation zones (NHK 2013b).

Unlike the Hiroshima Atomic Bomb Dome, the Kanto Earthquake Memorial Museum, and the Nojima Fault Preservation Museum, the 3.11 ruins are located in rural towns which were not popular destinations for tourists before the disaster. Media coverage of the disaster, coupled with the ongoing radiation leaks at Fukushima Daiichi Nuclear Power Plant, have made many feel travelling to this region would be dangerous (Imaoka 2013).

The Tôhoku Tourism Promotion Organisation (TTPO) has been making significant efforts to dispel any rumours suggesting that travel to the area is unsafe and instead promotes the region as a source of disaster education. One way in which they achieve this is through seminars for school personnel and travel agents in Tokyo and elsewhere, introducing participants to education programs that 'invite students to Tôhoku to learn about the disaster from guides trained as professional storytellers, building their awareness of disaster prevention' (Suma 2012).[6] In this way, TTPO is transforming disaster tourism or 'dark tourism' into something more than just the novelty of experiencing the 'sublime' (Weisenfeld 2012), but actually re-conceptualising the disaster sites into a collective hub for tourists interested in disaster prevention education.

Due to the scale and rarity of the 3.11 tsunami, it is also understandable that many scholars from all over the World who study such events may find the affected areas of particular interest. Cities and towns which decide to preserve their ruins may find that they are a popular destination for such researchers as well as school groups.

It will be significant to observe whether or not TTPO continues to promote the region as a collective of sites rather than as individual sites. As monuments that stand alone, the towns which decide to preserve their ruins would perhaps have less of a chance of attracting tourists than if they were to create some kind of pilgrimage in collaboration with neighbouring affected areas – each forming a piece of a larger story about the disaster. The National General Association for Stone Shops has already contributed to this idea of disaster heritage and pilgrimage in their creation of 500 new coastal stone monuments. In this way, the *tsunamihi* are supplementing the ruins as a path telling a story. It remains to be seen whether this approach to 3.11 monuments gains momentum as an officially endorsed policy. There is no doubt, however, that there is a widespread desire to be included in these developments. Even Urayasu City in Chiba Prefecture, for instance, has decided to monumentalise a few manholes uprooted when the soil liquefied during the earthquake.

Whether or not these ruins will bring vitality to the region remains to be seen. With economic losses at US$210 billion, 3.11

was the costliest natural disaster of all time (Guha-Sapir et al. 2012). Many residents are leaving or have left the disaster affected areas already. It will be important to study the response to these monuments in the coming years, so that when the next tsunami comes people will have learned from the successes and failures of the post-3.11 recovery. The costs to preserve and maintain the sites will be great and, because there has not been a precedent with which to compare, there is no telling how popular they might actually be amongst tourists, or whether it is even feasible to think the ruins will withstand the wear of time until the next great tsunami. In such an uncertain future are these risks worth it when the money could be spent on other things?

Conclusion

Throughout Japan's history of erecting *tsunamihi* monuments to tsunami disasters a progression can be observed through the messages inscribed on their surface, their content developing from the religious to the increasingly scientific and educational. With changing social attitudes, scientific knowledge, and technological capability, *tsunamihi* continue to evolve, and new forms of memorialization are also developing. *Tsunamihi* are clearly accepted within Japanese society as a tradition passed down over generations, and even when integrating new technologies they refer to a familiar model seen to fulfil a useful social and cultural function. In the aftermath of 3.11, however, there has also been a push to preserve ruins as monuments amongst the affected communities, a significant new chapter in people's adaptive processes to tsunami disasters. This step is driven by people's desire to improve disaster prevention awareness, as well as to help boost the economies of the affected areas through tourism. Unlike the *tsunamihi*, however, monuments created through the preservation of ruins attract great controversy. Further observation and research in the coming years, or even decades, will be significant to understanding if this monumentalisation of ruins successfully instils long-term tsunami disaster prevention awareness on a larger scale than the traditional *tsunamihi*, and whether and how this is integrated into Japanese disaster heritage.

Notes

[1] For more information on legends and inherited memories of past tsunamis a valuable source is Akenori Shibata's 'Importance of the inherited memories of great tsunami disasters in natural disaster reduction' presented at the proceedings of the International Symposium on Engineering Lessons Learned from the 2011 Great East Japan Earthquake, March 1–4, 2012, Tokyo, Japan.

[2] For instance, when the Shôka Earthquake of 1257 hit, the Pure Land Buddhist monk, Nichiren, proclaimed it punishment on the nation's ruler for not heeding his wisdom (De Wolf 2011).

[3] Before 1185, reading and writing education was restricted to the aristocracy and Buddhist monks who generally resided in the capitals of Nara (710–795) and Kyoto (795–1185). After 1185, education was extended to the wealthy samurai, or military class. In 1603 the capital was moved from western Japan to Edo (modern day Tokyo) and the Edo period (1603–1867) began. This is considered to be a relatively peaceful period in Japanese history in which literacy began to increase more rapidly and to spread more widely than before. Schools began to appear which included children from the samurai class as well as those of peasants and merchants (Deal 2006).

[4] In 1878, Ichizô Hattori investigated and compiled a list of destructive earthquakes from 416 to 1872. He realized that massive earthquakes tended to occur in groups (Davison 1927:

178). Tatsuo Usami (1979) of the Earthquake Research Institute believes that this was probably the first study of its kind in Japan. By 1880, the Japan Seismology Society was established as the first of its kind in the World (Davison 1927). Then in 1892, the Imperial Earthquake Investigation came about to study how to prevent disasters caused by Earthquakes (Usami 1979).

[5] In 2014 the town dismantled two buildings, while the future of the last building is still unclear as the time of writing.

[6] TTPO has also invited representatives from foreign media platforms and tourist agencies to visit tourist spots in Tôhoku and ensure accurate information is being communicated about the areas safety and what they have to offer visitors.

References

Asma, S 2011 Nuclear Disasters, Tsunamis, Buddhism. *Chicago Tribune*, 18 March. http://newsblogs.chicagotribune.com/religion_theseeker/2011/03/nuclear-disasters-tsunamis-buddhism.html (accessed on 1 September 2015).

Craft, L 2012 Japan's 'Angry Mayor' Makes Himself Heard. 29 April. www.cbsnews.com/news/japans-angry-mayor-making-himself-heard/ (accessed on 1 September 2015).

Davison, C 1927 *The Founders of Seismology*. Cambridge: Cambridge University Press.

Deal, W 2006 *Handbook to Life in Medieval and Early Modern Japan*. New York NY: Facts On File.

De Wolf, C 2011 Kashima and the Catfish: Letter from Japan. *Commonwealth Magazine*, 158(8): 10.

Fackler, M 2011 Tsunami Warnings, Written in Stone. *New York Times*, 20 April. www.nytimes.com/2011/04/21/world/asia/21stones.html (accessed on 1 September 2015).

Grayson, D and Sheets, P 1979 Volcanic Disasters and the Archaeological Record. In: Sheets, P and Grayson, D (eds.) *Volcanic Activity and Human Ecology*. New York: Academic Press. pp. 623–632.

Guha-Sapir, D, Vos, F, Below, R and Ponserre, S 2012 *Annual Disaster Statistical Review 2011: The Numbers and Trends*. Centre for Research on the Epidemiology of Disasters (CRED). http://cred.be/sites/default/files/2012.07.05.ADSR_2011.pdf (accessed on 1 September 2015).

Holguín-Veras, J 2012 Japan's 1,000-year-old Warning. *Los Angeles Times*, 11 March. http://articles.latimes.com/2012/mar/11/opinion/la-oe-holguin-veras-tsunami-20120311 (accessed on 1 September 2015).

Imaoka, L 2013 Repurposing Place Online: Japan's Push for Foreign Tourists after 3.11. In: Interdisciplinary Conversations about Fukushima & the NE Japan Disaster, University of California, Berkley, May 2013. http://fukushimaforum.wordpress.com/workshops/sts-forum-on-the-2011-fukushima-east-japan-disaster/manuscripts/session-4a-when-disasters-end-part-i/repurposing-place-online-japans-push-for-foreign-tourists-after-3-11/ (accessed on 1 September 2015).

Institute of Disaster Mitigation for Urban Cultural Heritage 2012 *Interactive Map of Miyagi Prefecture's Tsunami Stones*. www.rits-dmuch.jp/jp/project/tsunami_monument.html (accessed on 1 September 2015).

Japan ICOMOS National Committee 2011 *The Great East Japan Earthquake: Report on the Damage to Cultural Heritage*. Tokyo: Japan ICOMOS National Committee, www.icomos.org/publications/ICOMOS%20Japan-earthquake_report_20111120.pdf (accessed on 1 September 2015)

Kornbacher, K 2002 Horsemen of the Apocalypse: The Relationship between Severe Environmental Perturbations and Cultural Change on the North East Coast of Peru. In: Torrence, R and Grattan, J (eds.) *Natural Disasters and Cultural Change*. London: Routledge. pp. 204–234.

Lowenthal, D 1989 Material Preservation and its Alternatives. *Perspecta*, 25: 66–77.

Murakami, H 2008 *Nankai Jishin Wo Shiru Tokushimaken No Jishin, Tsunami Hi (Tokushima Prefecture's Earthquake and Tsunami Stones Relating to Nankai Great Earthquake)* Research Centre for Management of Disaster and Environment, the University of Tokushima. www.jishin.go.jp/main/

bosai/kyoiku-shien/13tokushima/material/tksm_22_3.pdf (accessed on 1 September 2015).

National Geographical Data Center. n.d. Significant Earthquakes Database. www.ngdc.noaa.gov/nndc/struts/form?t=101650&s=1&d=1 (accessed on 1 September 2015).

NHK 2013a Today's Close-up: Building Preservation: Lessons from the Tsunami. *NHK*, 15 May. www.nhk.or.jp/japan311/kuro-lessons.html (accessed on 1 September 2015).

NHK 2013b Tomorrow: Tourism That Tells a Story. *NHK*, 7 October. www.nhk.or.jp/japan311/tmrw2-tour.html (accessed on 1 September 2015).

Oliver-Smith, A 1986 *The Martyred City: Death and Rebirth in the Andes*. Albuquerque: University of New Mexico Press.

Oliver-Smith, A 1996 Anthropological Research on Hazards and Disasters. *Annual Review of Anthropology*, 25: 303–328.

Onagawa Town Reconstruction Development Committee 2011 Onagawa Town Reconstruction Plan (Draft) (Shiryô 1-2 Onagawachô fukkô keikaku (an)) [pdf] www.town.onagawa.miyagi.jp/hukkou/pdf/keikaku/04.kihonkeikaku.pdf (accessed on 1 September 2015).

Onishi, N 2012 As Japan Works to Patch Itself Up, a Rift Between Generations Opens. *New York Times*, 12 February. www.nytimes.com/2012/02/13/world/asia/amid-japan-reconstruction-generational-rift-opens.html (accessed on 1 September 2015).

Petzet, M 2003 Place-Memory-Meaning: Preserving Intangible Values in Monuments and Sites, paper presented at The ICOMOS 14th General Assembly and Scientific Symposium: 'Place-Memory-Meaning: Preserving Intangible Values in Monuments and Sites', Victoria Falls, Zimbabwe, 27–31 October 2003. www.international.icomos.org/victoriafalls2003/papers/4%20-%20Allocution%20Petzet.pdf (accessed on 1 September 2015).

Savage, K 2006 Trauma, Healing, and the Therapeutic Monument. *Public Art Review*, 35: 41–45.

Smits, G 2006 Shaking Up Japan: Edo Society and the 1855 Catfish Picture Prints. *Journal of Social History*, 39 (4): 1045–1078.

www.personal.psu.edu/faculty/g/j/gjs4/Shaking_Up_Japan.pdf (accessed on 1 September 2015).

Suma, T 2012 Tôhoku Tourism Current Situation and Reconstruction. Institute for International Studies and Training (IIST), 30 November. www.iist.or.jp/en-m/2012/0213-0870/ (accessed on 1 September 2015).

Tohkai Shimpo 2012a Discussing the Preservation and Dismantling of the "Message on the Wall" in Rikuzentakata's Chuo Community Centre. *Tohkai Shimpo,* 23 August.

Tohkai Shimpo 2012b Shiritsu Chûô Kôminkan No Messêji Shi Ni Hozon Motomeru Seigansho Teishutsu (Petition Seeking to Save the Message on the Wall of Rikuzentakata's Chûô Community Center). *Tohkai Shimpo,* 25 July.

Torrence, R. and Grattan, J 2002 *Natural Disasters and Cultural Change.* London: Routledge.

Usami, T 1979 Study of Historical Earthquakes in Japan. *Bulletin of the Earthquake Research Institute,* 54: 399–439.

Weisenfeld, G 2012 *Imaging Disaster: Tokyo and the Visual Culture of Japan's Great Earthquake of 1923.* Oakland, CA: University of California Press.

Weitzman, M 2011 First Japan Tsunami Monument has QR Code Video and Advice. *Digital Journal,* 23 December. http://digitaljournal.com/article/316636 (accessed on 1 September 2015).